Bibliografische Information Der Deutschen Bibliothek

Die Deutsche Bibliothek verzeichnet diese Publikation in der Deutschen
Nationalbibliografie; detaillierte bibliografische Daten sind im Internet über
http://dnb.ddb.de abrufbar.

ISBN 3-8325-1253-5

Logos Verlag Berlin
Comeniushof, Gubener Str. 47,
10243 Berlin
Tel.: +49 030 42 85 10 90
Fax: +49 030 42 85 10 92
INTERNET: http://www.logos-verlag.de

Benchmark

Integrated Performance Analysis of Computer Systems (IPACS) Benchmarks for Distributed Computer Systems

April 2006

Project Management:

Dr. Franz-Josef Pfreundt (Fraunhofer ITWM and Project Leadership)
Prof. Dr. Hans-Werner Meuer (University of Mannheim)
Dr.-Ing. habil. Alfred Geiger (T-Systems Solutions for Research GmbH)
Prof. Dr.-Ing. habil. Djamshid Tavangarian (University of Rostock)

Editors:

Michael Krietemeyer (michael.krietemeyer@uni-rostock.de)
Matthias Merz (merz@rz.uni-mannheim.de)

Authors:

Giovanni Falcone (falcone@rz.uni-mannheim.de)
Dr. Heinz Kredel (kredel@rz.uni-mannheim.de)
Sebastien Kreuter (skreuter@rumms.uni-mannheim.de)
Michael Krietemeyer (michael.krietemeyer@uni-rostock.de)
Dr. Dirk Merten (merten@itwm.fhg.de)
Martin Meuer (martin.meuer@rz.uni-mannheim.de)
Matthias Merz (merz@rz.uni-mannheim.de)
Dr. Franz-Josef Pfreundt (pfreundt@itwm.fhg.de)
David Reinig (dreinig@rz.uni-mannheim.de)
Henry Ristau (henry.ristau@uni-rostock.de)
Dr. Christian Simmendinger (christian.simmendinger@t-systems-sfr.com)
Daniel Versick (daniel.versick@uni-rostock.de)

The project, on which this report is based, was supported by funding of the Federal Ministry of Education and Research (BMBF). The funding identification numbers are listed in table 1. The authors are responsible for the content of this publication.

Project Partner	Funding Identification Number
Institut für Techno- und Wirtschaftsmathematik (ITWM)	01 IR B03 B
University of Mannheim, IT Center	01 IR B03 C
T-Systems Solutions for Research GmbH	01 IR B03 D
University of Rostock, Chair of Computer Architecture	01 IR B03 E

Table 1: Funding Identification Numbers

Foreword

When people speak about the performance analysis of computer systems, they often refer to simple benchmark tests that cover specific hardware characteristics. The well-known LINPACK benchmark for example, analyzes the floating point rate of execution for solving a linear system of equations. LINPACK summarizes different performance aspects (memory bandwidth and floating point operations) of a computer system to a single value (R_{max}). This allows building up a ranking system of HPC systems in an easy way, as it is demonstrated by the TOP500 supercomputer list. But summarizing performance of multiple categories into one score is highly subjective and could often be insufficient for an in-depth performance analysis.

New approaches cover major performance aspects of a computer. IDC, on the one hand, tries building a balanced rating system based on three categories (processor, memory, and interconnect performance). The HPC Challenges project, on the other hand, recommends the usage of six further benchmarks in addition to the LINPACK benchmark.

The IPACS project tries to provide a more comprehensive approach. The objective is to develop methods for measuring system performance on High Performance Computers based on low-level benchmarks, compute kernels, open source- and commercial application benchmarks. Additionally, IPACS covers the development of methods for performance modelling and prediction of commercial codes. In order to ensure an easy usability and a just-in-time analysis of benchmark results, the IPACS benchmarks are embedded into a benchmark environment consisting of a web based repository and a distributed benchmark-execution framework. By providing a new mechanism for an automatic installation and execution of benchmarks, IPACS also simplifies the performance analysis of computer system.

The IPACS client and execution framework as well as the IPACS benchmark suite are available for download at `www.ipacs-benchmark.org`. On this web site, you will also find our information retrieval component, that allows the search of benchmark results, the performance predication module as well as a kiviat diagram module, which allows an in-depth analysis of two or more high performance computers.

This book is structured into four parts: An introduction into the IPACS project, the results achieved by each project partner and a conclusion that identify future research topics. Finally, an appendix will provide a complete list of all IPACS publications and a comprehensive technical reference to the IPACS software environment.

IV

We thankfully acknowledge the fruitful discussions with our colleagues from the IPACS project and others. In particular, our team says thank you to Hàns-Werner Meuer, Djamshid Tavangarian, Alfred Geiger, and Erich Strohmaier for clarifying the requirements of the benchmark process. Our team also owes to thank all authors listed here for their work and the fact that they have kindly and actively supported our project and contributed to successfully finalizing this project. We appreciate and thank the executive director of the IT Center of the University of Mannheim, Hans-Günther Kruse, our colleges from the IT Center, the department of Information Systems III, and the Department of Mathematics and Computer Science of the University of Mannheim for their continuous support. Finally, we thank Klaus Thiele for improving the linguistic aspect of this publication.

The work on IPACS was supported by a grant from the German Federal Ministry of Education and Research (BMBF) in the program "High Performance and Grid Computing".

April 2006   Michael Krietemeyer and Matthias Merz

Contents

Part I

The IPACS Project

Chapter 1

IPACS Preface

With the continuing relevance of PC-clusters, SMP-clusters and the development of chip architectures into memory hierarchies and internal parallel processing, computer architectures have become more and more complex. Parallelism and the growing capacity of memory and storage have led to an increase of the growth of today's problems. But reliable and easy-to-use benchmarks, which moreover support the users in rating and evaluating parallel computer systems and help in the procurement of new computers, are still missing.

1.1   Context and Motivation

In this section, we will give some background information on performance analysis of computer systems before turning to related efforts in developments of integrated benchmarking environments.

With no doubt, the performance of computers, PCs and SMPs has been increased enormously in the last decades. This growth was driven not only by always raising clock rates but also by further developments of the chip architectures. Technologies like memory hierarchies, pipelines, or internal parallel processing and threading had significant impact. But these developments have also made computer architectures more and more complex and difficult to evaluate.

In addition to that, parallel clusters are widely used in the mean time and no longer restricted to a few HPC sites, enhancing the importance of parallelism and parallel performance for architectures as well as for programming techniques. This trend will become vitally in the near future since the increase of clock rates will reach its limit soon. With IBM's BlueGene/L, today already an architecture with a few ten-thousand processors is available. Even desktop machines will provide multiple cores, and with the new Cell architecture, a hybrid of cache and vector processors is on the market. Finally, with the implementation of computing and/or data grids, the meaning of distributed computing will be changed.

These developments immensely increase the complexity and variety of computer architectures. More and more, hardware features and components, like network connections and protocols for parallel computing, have to be taken into account in order to estimate, rate and understand the performance of a system. This has also led to an increase of the complexity and difficulty of measuring the performance with benchmarks.

On the other hand, the increasing performance of computer systems, together with the growing capacity of memory and storage, has also improved the applicability of these architectures. The size of problems that can be treated or solved with clusters has grown enormously as well as precision and accuracy. Computer simulations are a valuable tool in more and more areas. With this development, information about performance also becomes important for more and more users, increasing the impact of benchmarking results. But the interpretation of such results or even the execution of benchmarks by a larger group of users is hampered by the complexity and the variety of architectures and benchmarks.

Among the vast number of benchmark programs, the TOP500 [1] list, based on the LINPACK benchmark [2], is the most publicly visible benchmark in the world. Its success comes first from the open availability of the source and supporting code together with the community validation of the results, secondly from the scalability of the LINPACK bench-mark over all computer architectures within the last 25 years and thirdly from the interest of computer manufacturers in publishing the best LINPACK numbers for their systems as a competitive comparison. LINPACK numbers are for customers a prime corrective to the peek advertised performance (PAP) of computer systems, since a real benchmark program must be executed on an existing computer in order to obtain the performance numbers. Many other benchmark initiatives fail short on some of these three aspects:

- the benchmarks are only meaningful for certain architectures, hardware features or certain system sizes (e.g. NAS PB [3, 4] use only fixed problem sizes),

- to obtain and publish the benchmark one must be a member of an organization (and sometimes pay high membership fees) and follow certain procedures (e.g. SPEC [5]), TPC [6])

- or there is only an academic interest in the results of a benchmark (see the NETLIB link collection [2] with many dead projects).

However, the success of the LINPACK benchmark is also due to a limitation, it assesses the suitability of a computer system only by computing a solution to a dense and arbi-trarily big system of linear equations. But many of today's applications incorporate new algorithms with different system stress patterns or algorithms based on new mathemat-ical theories. Applications, which are not numerical and yet using parallel systems, are still not covered. With the growing relevance of computing grids, the situation will even become more aggravated in a few years. On the practical side, running the LINPACK with reasonable results by a benchmark professional is relatively easy, but for most new or young benchmarkers, it is very hard to tune and optimize the LINPACK software config-uration to achieve good results.

The IPACS project [7] wants to improve this situation by augmenting LINPACK with a set of low-level and application benchmarks and in easing the execution of these benchmarks. In cooperation with colleagues at LBNL/NERSC, IPACS wants to define a new basis for benchmarks measuring system performance of distributed systems. These benchmarks should allow a realistic evaluation of performance, leading even to the prediction of performance, and are especially designed to be scalable and portable in order to facilitate their wide range and future use. The evaluation and selection or the development of augmenting benchmarks is part of other IPACS publications [8, 7] and some extend in Section 3.2. The usability of these benchmarks is further improved by providing a benchmark execution environment with online evaluation of benchmarking results to assist the inexperienced user.

1.2   The Goal of IPACS

As described above, the main goals and efforts of the IPACS project go in two directions: The development and compilation of benchmarks that are adequate for the complexity of today's and future systems, and the easing of the execution of these benchmarks and the interpretation of their results for a wide group of users.

For these goals, the benchmarks, which are developed, tested and propagated, comply to the following fundamental qualities:

- Scalable: The problem size is adaptable for a broad class of systems and should also jut out the next 10 years (Petaflop systems).

- Portable: The benchmarks should be public available. Moreover, installing and starting the benchmarks should be possible in a simple way without special efforts.

- Realistic: The benchmarks provide a framework for measuring system performance in a realistic, expressive, universally valid way.

This will guarantee the usability of these benchmarks for a wide variety of systems and the usefulness of their results. Furthermore, these results are used in this project in order to create the basis for forecasting the system performance for commercial applications in a simple way and particularly support specifically the industrial users stronger.

To cover all the relevant performance aspects of an architecture, the benchmarks are organized in the following groups:

- Low level benchmarks for the characterization of the computer or the Grid condition

- Open source benchmarks for industry near applications,

- Scalable benchmarks for commercial codes.

Additionally, "non-numeric applications", whose behavior, until now, was hardly examined, shall also be taken into account. And, finally, grid benchmarks are developed, including the environment for connecting and addressing grid services. Based on a component architecture, the IPACS benchmarks are also used as basis for these grid benchmarks. With this benchmark compilation, performance data can be collected on all levels of a given system for the purpose of allowing a deep insight into all main performance aspects. This insight is additionally used to develop performance modeling techniques for commercial application. Based on the benchmark results characterizing a given architecture, a model is presented that allows predicting the performance of complex applications. While the precision of such predictions is limited to $\approx 10\%$, the technique is easy to apply and should support the (industrial) user in interpreting and transferring benchmark data to his needs.

The second goal and essential element of the new benchmark suite is the simple usability of the benchmark by the user. In order to simplify the benchmarking process, a new mechanism is provided to enable an automatic installation and execution of benchmarks. A benchmark client has been developed that automatically allows the download of components from a repository and enables the upload of the results on the attached web server in interaction with the user. In addition to that, the user is supported and guided in executing the benchmark, i.e. defining the necessary options, building a job and submitting it to a queuing system. The results will be presented automatically via a web repository, allowing an easy comparison, sorting and analysis. This shall increase the acceptance of the benchmarks and form a data basis for performance measurements of distributed systems, that are valuable for experienced benchmarkers as well as for users of applications and architectures.

1.3   Related Work

Other benchmarking activities do not aim at such a highly automated benchmarking process cycle. There is one project, 'Repository in a Box', (RIB, [9]), which is a software package for creating web meta-data repositories which can contain metadata for benchmark suites for various application domains. This tool helps finding benchmarks or other software in a specific application domain that does not contain the benchmark code or benchmark results. The PERFORMANCE DATABASE SERVER ([10]) is a webserver which contains results of various benchmarks from Dhrystone to Linpack. The results from Linpack are mostly up to date, but other tables contain merely historical data. Data input seems to be sent via email to the maintainers. The goal of the PERFORMANCE EVALUATION RESEARCH CENTER ([11]) is a scientific understanding and improvement of the performance of HPC systems. Although they develop benchmarks and performance models for predictions (just as IPACS), facilitating the benchmarking and publishing process seems not to be intended. The HPC CHALLENGE ([12]), together with the PAMAC project ([13]) also aim at a suitable benchmark suite which can comple-

ment the Linpack/TOP500 benchmark. The proposed benchmarks are primarily based
on Linpack and its software infrastructure. The suite has not defined an I/O benchmark
and there are no application benchmarks. The web-site contains an archive of benchmark
results and provides a web-form to be filled out and submitted together with the benchmark result file. User validation is via email response with an activating URL. So the
IPACS concept of integrating a benchmark code repository, a benchmark result repository and an automated process cycle contributes new ideas and experiences in the field
of benchmarking.

Chapter 2

The IPACS Project

2.1 IPACS Project Partners

In this section, the IPACS project partners, namely Fraunhofer Institut für Techno- und Wirtschaftsmathematik (ITWM), University of Mannheim (IT Center), T-Systems Solutions for Research GmbH and University of Rostock (Chair of Computer Architecture), will be introduced briefly. The Pallas GmbH, which was acquired by Intel Corp. in 2003, was also an IPACS project partner until the date of its acquisition.

2.1.1 Institut für Techno- und Wirtschaftsmathematik (ITWM)

Since its foundation in 1995, the Institut für Techno- und Wirtschaftsmathematik (ITWM) at Kaiserslautern is intensively involved in the development and optimization of parallel applications in a variety of fields, such as fluid dynamics, transport processes, financial mathematics or visualization. As the first mathematical institute in the Fraunhofer-Society, the ITWM's assignment is in building a connection between mathematical research and practical applications. Therefore, the close relationship with the Department of Mathematics with the Technical University of Kaiserslautern is especially important for the ITWM. It has become one of the leading partners providing mathematical research in industry.

The main tools in order to achieve this aim are effective algorithms and computer simulations with increasing importance due to the ever growing power of computer systems and clusters. In particular, parallelization and distributed computing is in the focus of the activity. This includes the development of new, highly parallel applications as well as parallelization frameworks. For this purpose it maintains a coupled system of PC-clusters of different architectures for research and development.

Applications have been developed in the fields of e.g. fluid dynamics, molecular dynamics and structural mechanics, which are in regular use for internal research as well as industrial projects. Two of these applications, the lattice Boltzmann code PARPAC and the structural mechanics code DDFEM, are also used as benchmarks in the IPACS project.

The development of effective parallel applications requires intensive benchmarking, code instrumentation and performance analysis. The knowledge in these areas is shared in cooperations with industrial partners by parallelizing and optimizing existing software for high performance systems and specific architectures.

With the construction of the Fraunhofer Resource Grid (FhRG), the ITWM is also involved in the implementation of a grid infrastructure and thereby in shaping the distributed computing environment of the future.

2.1.2 University of Mannheim, IT Center

The University of Mannheim is widely recognized for its excellence in business, economics, sociology, psychology, and political since. Research and teaching are closely interrelated in all subject areas and further fields of research - law, humanities, mathematics, and computer science - are woven into these disciplines in a unique way.

The University of Mannheim's IT Center (RUM) provides its services to approximately 12,000 students and all scientific institutions and research facilities at the university. Among others, the IT Center offers advanced computing resources in order to enable computationally-intensive research and conducts research in the field of high performance computing and parallel processing.

In 1986, Prof. Dr. Meuer initiated and organized the first Mannheim Super Computer Seminar, which has evolved into the annually held International Supercomputer Conference (ISC). Today, it has grown and become one of the most important supercomputer events in Europe and enjoys international recognition. The ISC addresses the topics applications, architectures and HPC trends and is directed to users, operators and manufacturers of high performance computers. It features up to date information from practitioners, researchers and educators to the needs for decision makers and planners of information systems.

The University of Mannheim, together with the University of Tennessee and LBNL/ NERSC, have been assembling and maintaining the "Top 500 Supercomputer List" since June 1993. The list represents the 500 most efficient and powerful computer systems in the world and is compiled twice a year. Because statistics on high-performance computers are of major interest to manufacturers, users, and potential users, the list has proved to be an important instrument to the judgement of the HPC market.

Together with the Interdisciplinary Center for Scientific Computing of the University of Heidelberg (IWR), the University of Mannheim's IT Center has installed a parallel high-performance computer consisting of 512 AMD Athlon MP processors in order to enable computationally-intensive research.

2.1.3 T-Systems Solutions for Research GmbH

T-Systems is one of Europe's leading providers of information and communications technology (ICT). Within the *Deutsche Telekom* group, T-Systems is responsible for serving major business accounts. The company has some 41,000 staff in more than 20 countries on its payrolls .

T-Systems' solutions improve the competitiveness of the business its customers in the industry sectors telecommunications, services and finance, public and healthcare as well as manufacturing. For its customers, the company optimizes processes, cuts costs and improves earnings, making targeted use of industry expertise and cutting-edge technology. Its services range from the integration of new ICT solutions into existing customer systems, through the implementation and operation of desktop systems, data centers and networks, all the way to telecommunications services and solutions for international carriers.

T-Systems' services encompass all levels of the information and communications technology value chain, spanning from ICT infrastructure and ICT solutions, up to and including business process management. T-Systems-SfR is a joint-venture between T-Systems International (75%) and the DLR, the German Center for Aerospace Research (25%). T-Systems-SfR has a focus on services for industrial and public Research and Development. T-Systems-SfR forms the Business-Center for the R&D market of T-Systems-International (TSI) and is fully integrated into the TSI structures.

T-Systems is a partner in the *hww* consortium (High Performance Computing for Science and Industry), the joint company for supercomputer operations of T-Systems, Porsche and the universities of Stuttgart, Karlsruhe and Heidelberg.

2.1.4 University of Rostock, Chair of Computer Architecture

The Chair of Computer Architecture is specialized in Internet architectures with focus on internet-based high-performance data processing and multimedia Learning Management Systems for wireless and wired communication networks as well as distributed embedded systems. Different architectures have been developed or optimized for local and wide-area communication networks, their organizational mechanisms with regard to different applications tested, and new management procedures designed. These have been introduced with very good response, nationally and internationally. Current developments and research works includes different projects regarding:

- wireless communication architectures for voice and data transfer with use of standardized technologies like Wi-Fi, WiMAX, GSM, UMTS

- distributed computer architectures based on local and wide area communication networks

- open source in embedded systems

- XML-based Learning Management Systems for eLearning systems

Focusing the IPACS project, the following developments are of particular interest. Within the Hypercomputing project, a solution for network-based and Internet Computing has been developed. The Hypercomputer represents a distributed computational resource implementing various methods for system management and security. A distributed resource management, a prediction for available resources and a transparent job and data management are a few important issues of the developed system. The project is not only concentrated on the research of network based computing, but also on the tools being developed and made available, which would ensure an easy use and administration of the system in a wide spread infrastructure.

Knowledge in the area of workstation cluster was extended by the development of the network architectures CNA and Fast CNA (Concurrent Network Architecture). Furthermore, competence in associative storage concepts has been extended by the development of an associative storage architecture for computing grids within the IPACS project.

2.1.5   Pallas GmbH – A Former Project Partner

Pallas GmbH was an independent IT company in the ExperTeam Group. They worked with reputable national and international organizations in the field of IT consulting, IT solutions, services, and software products for high performance computing, GRID computing, internet security, and knowledge management. From 1991 to 2003, the staff of Pallas has grown up to 50 highly competent IT experts.

In the HPC area, Pallas developed and distributed software solutions for High Performance Computing (HPC) platforms. As the international market leader, they worked with important users and vendors of technical HPC computing. For applications in the commercial area, they had offered consulting services for performance quality assurance to guarantee the performance of complex IT systems and applications.

The Intel Corp. acquired the high-performance computing group of Pallas GmbH, in an effort to bolster its clustering expertise. Therefore, the former HPC business of Pallas has become part of Intel Corporation since September, 2003. This acquisition has provided Intel critical High Performance Computing technology and engineering expertise for Intel Xeon and Itanium processor families. The transaction includes the acquisition of intellectual property and 23 employees from Pallas GmbH. Pallas proceeds working in the Security and Intelligence divisions with no change.

The acquisition of Pallas GmbH by the Intel Corp. has strong effects on the IPACS project. From the project start up to 2003, Pallas acted as project leader and was involved in the development of the IPACS client and some of the IPACS benchmarks. Because of the BMBF's policies, only small and medium sized enterprises (SMEs) are funded. And since Intel Corp. is a large scale enterprise, Intel was not able to continue Pallas' work. As a result, the project schedule and accessible achievements have been delayed due to Pallas' retiring.

2.2 IPACS Work Packages

The IPACS project consists of several work packages that address specific problem areas that need to be solved in order to achieve the objectives mentioned in Section 1.2. Besides project management, which was part of the Fraunhofer ITWM, these work packages are:

2.2.1 Open Source Application Benchmarks

Based on existing codes, practical and scalable benchmarks for areas like fluid dynamics, image processing and others will be developed as open source codes. The scalability, which is necessary to run huge problems using the complete system environment is a major characteristic for these benchmarks. They will help to gain information about the usage of the memory hierarchy, the network, the CPU and the I/O system. The intent is understanding the sources of performance problems.

Primarily responsible for this work package are Fraunhofer ITWM and T-Systems. Additionally, the University of Mannheim is jointly responsible for the development of a data mining benchmark.

2.2.2 Low-Level Benchmarks

The purpose of low-level benchmarks is the evaluation of characteristics (signatures) of computer systems. Included are compute benchmarks (LINPACK), communication benchmarks (B_{eff}), I/O benchmarks as well as benchmarks which characterize the underlying memory hierarchy. In order to use these benchmarks within the intended architecture of components (grid benchmark), the I/O interfaces have to be taken particularly into consideration. There is a separate working package, which deals with I/O benchmarks. The decisive factor is, that low-level benchmarks lead to a characterization of computer systems.

Primarily responsible for this work package is the Fraunhofer ITWM.

2.2.3 I/O Benchmarks

Up to now, the evaluation of distributed computer systems has neglected the I/O performance. Therefore, concepts for measuring and evaluating the I/O performance of distributed computer systems will be developed. These concepts will build the basis for the development of measuring methods (if necessary with the use of MPI-IO interfaces), which should characterize computer systems as low-level benchmarks. I/O concepts in the area of PC-clusters and computing grids are still not matured; thus, current developments have to be taken into account.

Primarily responsible for this work package is the University of Rostock.

2.2.4   Benchmarks for Commercial Applications

Scalable benchmarks will be developed for a variety of commercial applications (Fluent, Magmasoft, LS-Syna, etc.). The intent is evaluating software-specific characteristics (e.g. data flow-rate), which are independent of manufacturers, and to put them at industrial user's disposal. At least two software packages of different areas should be treated. The validity of the benchmarks should be verified within a real production environment in cooperation with the users. Hence, the work is focussing at first on the conception of benchmark examples. The test of the software manufacturers will build the foundation of the benchmarks.

Primarily responsible for this work package are Fraunhofer ITWM and T-Systems.

2.2.5   Performance Prediction Methods

The results of the performance and the analysis of the previous working packages represent the context between the characteristics of the computer systems and of the applications. The goal of this working package is collecting enough information in order to picture this context in a mathematical manner with the use of system identification methods. At first, models of neuronal grids will be used. The purpose is making predictions for the tested commercial software packages based on the low-level benchmarks only. The results of this working package should lead to a performance prediction tool for commercial software.

Primarily responsible for this work package is Fraunhofer ITWM.

2.2.6   Grid Benchmarks

Within the framework of this working package, a grid benchmark as well as the technology for grid-adaptive applications will be developed. The task of a grid benchmark is analyzing and parameterizing the grid environment at first, followed by the customization and the execution of the benchmark. The benchmarks, which have been developed within the first three working packages, are available from a benchmark repository and will be used from the benchmark infrastructure under development. These benchmarks are a basis for the further development and optimization of grid products.

Primarily responsible for this work package is Fraunhofer ITWM. Additionally, T-Systems is jointly responsible for the evaluation of the gird benchmarks in different environments.

2.2.7   Benchmark Environment

The execution of benchmarks should be simplified. Therefore, a benchmark client will provide the essential configuration tasks. The client connects to a web-based repository, which contains all benchmarks as source code and as binaries for a variety of architectures. The purpose of the client is detecting the local configuration of the computer in interaction with the user, determining the type of test, loading the necessary sources and binaries and, finally, publishing the benchmark results on the web server.

This new approach of the execution of performance analysis should substitute the current tests, which last several weeks. It will also provide the user with detailed system analysis and performance prediction, not only MFLOP values.

Besides the development of application benchmark, the development of the benchmark environment is the most important working package within the IPACS project. The evaluation of the system configuration, the generation of the locally executable binaries and security matters makes this work so difficult.

Primarily responsible for this work package is the University of Mannheim.

2.2.8 Instrumentation Library

Today's leading analysis tools for parallel applications, *Vampir* and *Vampirtrace*, are supplied by the IPACS project partner Pallas. Vampir provides a basic analysis of the communication of the inspected software. The purpose of this working package is providing a complete analysis of the software, so that the trace files will contain all relevant information. The analysis of the benchmark measurements will be automized and standardized.

Primarily responsible for this work package are Fraunhofer ITWM and T-Systems.

2.2.9 Web Server, Workshops and Public Relations

An essential element of the IPACS project is the interaction with hardware manufacturers, software developers and users of high-performance computers. In order to ensure the neutrality of IPACS, these groups will not be integrated as project partners. Instead, the integration should rather take place in the context of two annual workshops carried out as well in coordination with us. The target group mentioned above shall be appealed to and tied by intensive public relations and a web portal.

The web portal's acceptance by benchmark users is very important. These users are enterprises or the public sector, who want to confirm their hardware selection with performance data, but also scientists and software manufacturers. Therefore, the conception of the web portal is of particular importance. The simultaneous function as Benchmark repository establishes a connection to a database which permits a simple reorganization of the repository.

The IPACS results will be discussed in two annual workshops. Because of the fact that the IPACS project partners have no access to all world-wide available hardware architectures, the assistance of scientists and developers from all areas is important. This shall essentially happen on a voluntary basis. In order to reduce costs, these workshops shall be integrated into the supercomputer conferences taking place every year in the USA and Germany. Moreover, this will have a positive effect on the number of participants of the workshops.

Primarily responsible for this work package is the University of Mannheim.

2.2.10   Benchmarking

The execution of benchmarks with the use of the developed software is a necessary and essential part of the IPACS project. Existing computer systems of the project partners will be used as well as relevant external systems. Therefore the cooperation with the American groups will be very advantageous. The early inclusion of users should lead to a higher acceptance and quality assurance. Moreover, substantial contributions of the performance data should be provided by the users.

Primarily responsible for this work package are all project partners.

2.2.11   I/O Performance, Associative Storage Concepts

The results of the third working package (I/O benchmarks) will lead straight to suggestions of an approvement of the I/O performance of today's systems. Associative and adaptive storage concepts should be evaluated on the basis of the benchmark analysis of existing storage concepts. A prototype will be implemented on a PC-cluster.

Primarily responsible for this work package is the University of Rostock.

Chapter 3

IPACS Framework

3.1 The Benchmarking Environment

Due to the continuing relevance of High Performance Computing, there is an increasing need for people in research labs, institutes and high-tech companies, e.g. decision-makers interested in buying a new supercomputer, of getting above all up-to-date performance information about specific computer systems. As outlined in section 3.2, performance aspects can be gained in an objective way, by using the IPACS benchmark suite. In order to support the execution of benchmarks, a benchmark environment has been developed that also allows users to provide their measured results to third parties. Therefore, the benchmark client submits these information to the web based repository server and all benchmark results can be accessed through dynamically generated web pages just-in-time. The information displayed on this pages is not a single ranking for a specific benchmark as it is done with the LINPACK benchmark on the TOP500 list. Furthermore, it enables a user to see the strengths of his own system in comparison to others as well as to detect bottlenecks and potential problems. As already mentioned PRIOMARK (see chapter 3.2.1.1) analyzes the file system and disk I/O performance, PMB (see chapter 3.2.1.2) the load of the interconnection between different nodes and CACHEBENCH (see chapter 3.2.1.2) the memory bandwidth of cache hierarchies.

In the following subsections, we will introduce the benchmarking environment a little more in depth by first recalling a non-computer-assisted benchmarking process cycle. Furthermore, we shall outline the benchmark client as an essential part of the benchmark execution framework. Later on we will discuss the process how data is shared with the benchmark repository and finally, how interested parties like decision-makers are able to retrieve characteristic information as basis for reasonable investment decisions.

3.1.1 The Process of Benchmarking High Performance Computers

In recent years, it has become more evident that the process of benchmarking High Performance Computers is quite complex and requires fundamental benchmarking ex-

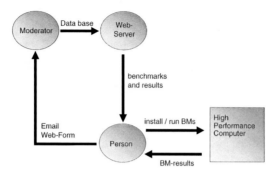

Figure 3.1: Non-Computer-Assisted Benchmarking Process Cycle.

perience. In particular, a benchmarker has to configure and compile benchmark sources with approved compiler flags and advanced operating system settings. Figure 3.1 recalls a non-computer-assisted benchmarking process cycle by the example of LINPACK: a person selects the LINPACK source code from NETLIB web-site, the LINPACK is transferred to the target computer system, compiled, tuned and by the benchmarker-executed without any computer-assistance. Finally, the results are pasted into a web-form at TOP500 or sent by email to the developer and maintainer of the benchmark. If the results are meaningful, wrong or bad can be seen by feedback from the TOP500 team or the biyearly published and moderated result lists on www.top500.org.

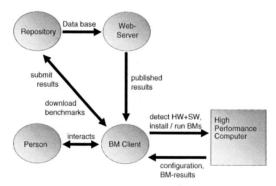

Figure 3.2: IPACS Process Cycle.

IPACS aims at an automated process cycle (see figure 3.2). The benchmark environment guides benchmarking professionals as well as unexperienced benchmarkers in selection, deployment, execution and tuning of benchmarks as well as in the comparison of measurement results with other computer systems. In detail, the benchmark client connects to the IPACS repository and guides a user in gathering basic facts about the corresponding High Performance Computer. Based on these information the repository server determines appropriate benchmark versions for the specific system and ensures an automatic download of the corresponding files. The benchmark client assists the user in compilation (if necessary), tuning and executing a selected benchmark. Once measurement results are available, they will be transmitted as XML form to the repository server. Finally the client guides the web-based browsing and comparison of the results in the information retrieval component (see section 3.1.4).

3.1.2 IPACS Client and Execution Framework

The IPACS benchmark client is, as part of the benchmark execution framework, the entry point for persons, companies, or manufacturers, which want to work with the IPACS benchmark environment. After a simple installation process via Java WebStart or a self extracting Java Archive File (IPACSClient.jar), the client software ends the installation process with an installation wizard, where the user finally needs to add extra information like the connection type to the internet.

The benchmarking environment provides, besides the source code of the different benchmarks, also binary versions for different system environments. In order to get an appropriate binary version of a benchmark and also for displaying the results of an accomplished benchmark regarding to results of other systems, some additional information about the measured one are needed. If the auto-detection mode is enabled, the client will automatically try to discover the needed information about the current system environment e.g. the current operating system. A simple script enables the user to additionally analyze an environment on a remote computer, if for example, a connection to the system to be measured is only available using a gateway computer. If the auto detection mode is enabled the output file gets automatically added to the client containing the results. Additionally relevant information about the site or the contact person of the measured system still need to be added manually.

The benchmark execution framework can be separated in two major parts: the benchmark client, which acts as a mediator between the user and the benchmark repository and the execution part handling the installation and execution of the available benchmarks.

The benchmark client has different roles in the benchmark environment. It's used to gather needed system information and also for collecting the benchmark results, transforming them to an XML File regarding to the IPACS specific DTD and sending them to the benchmark repository. In case the client is running on the system to be measured, it provides an interface which is the association to the second part, the benchmark execution, which can be run as a stand-alone.

The benchmark execution part enables a user to execute downloaded benchmarks, by compiling and tuning the source code on a specific system, almost without user interaction (figure 3.3). Before execution, standardized settings are made for the benchmarks, so that results delivered are comparable to the other ones available at the IPACS bench-

mark repository. For example, the installation and standardized execution of the HP
LINPACK benchmark is already available and other benchmarks will follow soon.

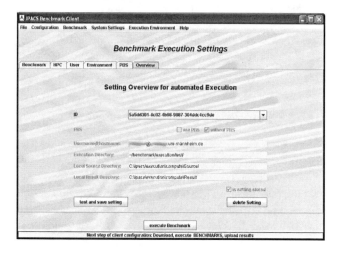

Figure 3.3: IPACS Execution Framework Overview.

3.1.3   IPACS Repository

The benchmark repository acts as central source of information for people interested in benchmarking High Performance Computers like scientists, administrators,
end-users, manufacturers, or decision-makers. It offers information about registered
high-performance computers, e.g. site information, common computer details as well as
technical parameters depending on the hard- and software environment. Moreover the
repository provides a database to collect and manage the benchmark results for every
benchmark type of the IPACS benchmark suite. All this information is accessible via
the IPACS website (www.ipacs-benchmark.org).

    Without being noticed by the benchmarker, the repository server provides essential
services to the IPACS benchmark client. Therefore, the repository server enables e.g.
the transmission of a current computer configuration together with a specific benchmark
result from the client. For detailed information about the IPACS repository, confer to
section 5.3.

3.1.4   Web-Presentation and Information Retrieval Component

Doing an investment in a supercomputer requires fundamental knowledge about hardware architectures and application software solutions in High Performance Computing.
Decision-makers e.g. interested in buying a new supercomputer are often not in the

Figure 3.4: Information Retrieval Screen at `www.ipacs-benchmark.org`.

proper position of expressing all technical requirements in a precise way. This is not to question the authority of a HPC center director, who will be able to meet investment decisions very well even without benchmark lists. Nevertheless, IPACS could provide a valuable assistance for decision-makers in the consideration of individual alternatives e.g. in enterprises and research facilities. Additionally, scientists might often specify their needs exactly regarding to software for mathematical models in order to perform complex simulations like weather forecast, automobile design and financial or economic models of behavior. But it remains an open question which computer architecture, interconnection or system software are best suited to solve these problems.

If decision-makers do not want to rely on the data of computer manufacturers, the best solution would be running the applications used under real conditions on different supercomputers. However, this seems to be an unrealistic choice as, on the one hand, supercomputers are not generally accessible for anybody or on the other hand, novel supercomputers are not yet constructed. A common solution is using a different kind of benchmarks that could reflect the real applications as realistically as possible. Even if it is not possible to run them directly on different supercomputers - using the IPACS repository data base to gather measurement results on a variety of architectures could be an appropriate solution. Additionally, the prediction models focused in section 3.3 enables performance modeling of not yet built computers from available prototypes.

One controversial subject in the presentation of the results is the order in which the computer systems are listed. For LINPACK/TOP500 , the computers are easily ordered with respect to their R_{max} (maximal LINPACK performance achieved in Gigaflops) value.

But with more than one different benchmark, it is not possible to find a meaningful way of ordering the systems. The International Data Corporation (IDC) [14] tries to define a rank based on an (equal) weighting scheme of the different benchmarks to construct a single number for ordering. However, there has been disagreement about this scheme in the scientific benchmark community [15] as a weight between different performance numbers depends on particular application characteristics. Each visitor has his own applications which imply different importance (or weights) between the numbers of different benchmarks. Therefore, IPACS will not imply any ordering on the overview results, but will provide decision-makers with the option of selecting their own ordering schemes for assessment.

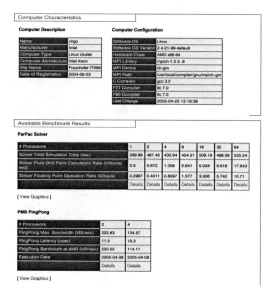

Figure 3.5: Result-Details.

The information retrieval screen, as shown in figure 3.4, is organized as easily as possible. In order to receive relevant benchmark results, decision-makers just have to select a set of benchmarks and make some restrictions regarding to manufacturer, computer type, computer architecture, operating system and hardware class. With this information, a table will be created representing the results together with a short computer description and the current computer-configuration. The results can be compared and sorted according to different benchmark columns. If someone is interested in more details about a special benchmark result, with a click on *view* the benchmark output will be displayed for documentation and verification (see figure 3.5).

The web interface is moreover integrated with the benchmark client. When a new benchmark result is uploaded to the repository, the client will open a comparison page,

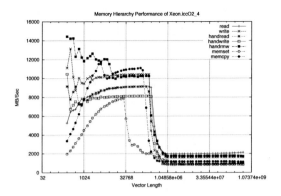

Figure 3.6: CACHEBENCH.

where this results will be listed in a table together with other known results for this benchmark. This allows an instantaneous comparison of personal benchmark results with other people's results. If the result numbers are below the current best results from others, the benchmark can be further tuned, rerun and uploaded again until satisfactory results are achieved. In case a benchmark doesn't reach an expected result after a comprehensive tuning, one could draw the conclusion that the examined computer architecture is not too well-suited for this specific class of applications. Besides tabular information, there are online graphics directly generated from the repository content for one benchmark (and one computer-configuration) over all known processor numbers. With this visual information, benchmarkers can easily identify weak scalability or problems with certain processor numbers and it also may be helpful for decision-makers in gaining a better insight. If a benchmark provides additional, more detailed graphics, e.g. CACHEBENCH or PRIOMARK, the corresponding pictures will be generated on the server side after uploading the results automatically. This frees the benchmarker from the installation of additional graphic software like gnuplot or netpbm (see figure 3.6). In the future, IPACS will also provide visualizations for different computers for several benchmarks (and certain processor numbers).

3.2   IPACS Benchmark Suite

The development and compilation of the IPACS benchmark suite is driven by the aim of providing a framework for measuring system performance in a realistic, expressive, universally valid way. Hence, it is not restricted to pure architectural benchmarks. But, in addition to that, the numbers measured should be related more or less directly to performance of real-world applications and throughput in production runs. Therefore, the collection of benchmarks is actually divided into four classes, which form a hierarchy

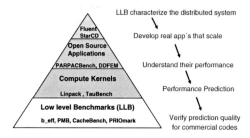

Figure 3.7: The 'Benchmark pyramid' illustrates the hierarchy of benchmarks and the utilization of the gathered information up to performance modeling.

depending on the complexity of the execution and the level of the measured data, as illustrated by the benchmark pyramid in figure 3.7.

These classes range from Low-level benchmarks, which measure basic performance aspects of a specific part of the architecture, through compute kernels to benchmarks for open-source and commercial applications, where the performance of a complex software package is determined. And, in addition to that, specific grid benchmarks are provided that measure the performance of tasks and processes common for grid usage and grid applications. In the selection of all these benchmarks, the scalability of the software has been an important criterion in order to ensure the applicability for future systems. With this variety the resulting suite covers a larger range of performance aspects than most other collections ([12], [5]) and provides the data necessary for the analysis of performance on all system levels. In the following, these classes and the benchmarks belonging to them are described in more detail.

3.2.1   Low-Level Benchmarks

The benchmarks in this class are intended to extract basic performance properties of the key components and devices of an architecture, i.e. the memory hierarchy, the file I/O system and the parallel network (the floating point unit, which mostly is not the bottleneck in today's systems, is evaluated by the compute kernels more accurately). For this, a collection of simple operations, basic access patterns and typical workloads are implemented and invoked in isolation. In detail, these benchmarks are PRIOMARK, CACHEBENCH and PMB.

3.2.1.1   PRIOMARK - Parallel I/O Benchmark

Modern computer systems use a hierarchical storage architecture called memory hierarchy, typically consisting of CPU registers as highest level followed by the 1st level cache, the 2nd level cache, the main memory, and secondary storage in form of hard disks. The performance gap between main memory and secondary storage of computer systems is the largest and increased continuously during the last years. Therefore, the analysis of secondary storage performance becomes very important and is a major element of low level benchmarks in the IPACS project.

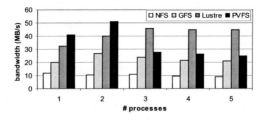

Figure 3.8: The cumulative bandwidth for different file systems against the number of processes on dual Pentium III cluster with Gigabit Ethernet interconnection, as measured with PRIOMARK

Operating systems organize secondary data storage into hierarchical structures called file systems and provide a file system interface to access data. The most common file system interface is the POSIX-I/O interface, designed to support file systems on local storage devices. Unfortunately it lacks support for parallel accesses to files in distributed environments. Other interfaces like the MPI-IO interface are developed to overcome this disadvantage and to allow parallel I/O in such environments [16].

File system benchmarks are applications to evaluate the performance of accesses to files in file systems. They measure the performance of read and write accesses. Since small attention was payed to I/O benchmarks in the past, there are few well known I/O benchmarks like Bonnie [17], IOzone [18], and B_{eff_io} [19]. The HPC CHALLENGE benchmark suite [12] does not contain an I/O benchmark at all. Available file system benchmarks lack in support for complex workload definitions or support one file system interface only. We implemented the novel I/O benchmark PRIOMARK in order to solve all these issues. PRIOMARK measures POSIX-I/O as well as MPI-IO interface calls and supports complex workload definitions describing the I/O access behavior of an application. By supporting user-defined workloads, the emulation of I/O activity of common applications is possible [20]. Furthermore, the PRIOMARK is based on an easily extensible plugin software architecture. It allows building of special versions, for example a non-parallel benchmark for stand-alone workstations or an only-parallel variant for clusters.

PRIOMARK supports two different performance analysis methods: Concurrent accesses of many processes to one common file and accesses to individual files of the processes. Both methods use the POSIX-I/O interface for performance evaluation. Furthermore, the individual file-per-process benchmark can also run in stand-alone environments.

The more interesting measurement method for distributed systems and parallel programming is the concurrent access to a common file. Using this access type, PRIOMARK is able to measure the POSIX-I/O as well as the MPI-IO interface calls with its different variants (individual file pointer, shared file pointer, explicit offset; see [16] for details). Additionally, it uses available synchronous and asynchronous file system interface calls. Synchronous calls return when the whole operation is completed and asynchronous calls return immediately while doing the operation in background. In case MPI-IO is used, even collective interface calls invoked and coordinated by a group of processes, are possible. They allow an optimization of disk accesses, for example by ordering the different accesses in order to reduce hard disk seeks. Additionally, MPI file views can be analyzed allowing every process to see only its segments of a file.

As stated above, PRIOMARK supports detailed application-specific workloads. The workload used during benchmark runs is a very important issue for the interpretation of measurement results, because the results may vary in a large range. Workloads are characterized by a lot of parameters e.g. the number of processes that access data and how data is accessed. PRIOMARK features the specification of many of these parameters. For example it allows the user to specify a range of file/data sizes, a range of block sizes for I/O requests, the ratio between read and write requests, and the used file system interface calls. These definition abilities allow the reproduction of access behavior of many existing programs. The whole workload configuration is stored in a single file and allows an easy rerun of the benchmark with the same settings. For supporting the user in creating workload configuration files, PRIOMARK includes workloads for main application domains (e.g. web server, workstation, on line transaction processing).

The PRIOMARK produces detailed measurement output. In order to assist the user it displays various calculated short summaries for the described file access methods and combines these to one value. With this value it enables the user to compare different file systems, file system interfaces or workloads to find the best combination for his application.

For example, figure 3.8 shows some measured values for a read intensive workload to compare four different file systems: NFS (Network File System, [21]), GFS (Global File System, [22] [23]), Lustre 1.0.4 ([24]), and PVFS 1 (Parallel Virtual File System, [25]). The shown bandwidths are accumulated by all started processes when accessing a common file. When increasing the number of concurrent processes, the Lustre bandwidth increases and reaches a stable value, whereas the NFS bandwidth continuously decreases. After reaching their maximum I/O performance at two concurrently running processes, the bandwidth of PVFS and GFS continuously decreases, too.

3.2.1.2   CACHEBENCH , PMB and B_{eff}

CACHEBENCH [26], taken from the LLCBENCH benchmark collection (low-level Characterization Benchmarks), is a synthetic benchmark to measure the bandwidth of a (hierarchic) memory subsystem. A pre-allocated part of the memory is addressed by straight read, write and read-modify-write accesses repeatedly. Additionally, partly optimized versions of theses accesses allow an evaluation of compiler effects. PMB (Pallas MPI Benchmarks) is a comprehensive set of MPI benchmarks developed by Pallas [27] that measures the bandwidth and latency of different MPI communication patterns. These patterns range from point-to-point message-passing to collective operations. In addition to that, the effect of different groupings of the processors are taken into account. Derived from PMB is the effective bandwidth benchmark (B_{eff}), which measures the accumulated bandwidth of the communication network of parallel and/or distributed computing systems. The algorithm averages several message sizes and communication patterns in order to take into account the fact that short and long messages are transferred with different bandwidth values in real applications, leading to one effective bandwidth. For a more detailed description and example results of these benchmarks, we shall refer to the cited literature.

3.2.2 Compute Kernels

The major aspect of the benchmarks in this class is the performance of a specific algorithm, which is isolated or derived from (a category of) 'representative' applications. One example for this is the well-known LINPACK benchmark, which performs basic Linear Algebra operations. Additional compute kernels are implemented in TAUBENCH, a parallel pseudo benchmark. The respective kernels are derived from TAU – a Navier Stokes solver, which has been developed at the German Center for Aerospace Research (DLR). A major advantage of using compute kernels is the fact that – while still being easy to handle – these benchmarks not only evaluate the underlying hardware, but at the same time test the quality of the compiler suite available.

3.2.3 Application Benchmarks

More complex is the structure of application benchmarks. These are derived from real parallel applications combined with a generic benchmark case. These benchmarks will demonstrate the effect of the interplay of different hardware components with their characteristics as measured by the low-level benchmarks, resulting in the sustained performance of an application. Therefore, this kind of data, which is missing in low-level benchmark suites ([12] and [28]), complements and exceeds the information that is contained in hardware benchmarks.

The benchmarks of this class in the IPACS project, chosen as 'representatives' of their software category, are derived from two applications developed at the ITWM [29] and are provided as source. This allows to study the effect of compiler optimization and to even pinpoint architecture specific bottlenecks.

The first one, PARPACBENCH, is a flow simulation code for viscous fluids through complex three-dimensional porous structures. It is based on the generalized lattice Boltzmann method, describing the Navier-Stokes equations by simulating simplified particle dynamics. It is fully parallelized, making it a highly efficient code for large and complex applications. The automatic domain decomposition allows dynamic load balancing. The number of communication steps between the calculation nodes is optimized by colored

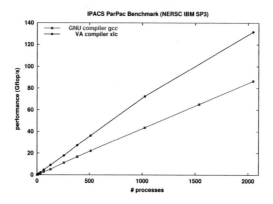

Figure 3.9: Measured speed-up of PARPACBENCH on an IBM SP3.

graph methods. As a benchmark case, the permeability of a generic cube with a regular internal structure is calculated.

The second one, DDFEM, is a parallel 3D linear elasticity solver for steady-state problems. Finite element discretization of tetrahedral meshes, which are generated by the built-in mesh generator, and first order shape functions are used to resolve the problem. An iterative linear solver-based on the conjugate gradients method with block-Jacobi preconditioning is employed. As a benchmark case, the deformation of a generic cylindric structure under an external normal force is calculated.

Both applications are implemented in C++, heavily using the object-oriented programming style. The benchmark geometries are generated by the application. Thereby, the size of the problem is scaled by the number of processors to keep a constant load per node and thus to receive a scalable benchmark. These more complex benchmark codes have been ported already to a great variety of architectures and have proven their scalability up to 1000 processors, as shown in figure 3.9.

3.2.4 Commercial Software Packages

Finally, the performance of commercial applications and software suites is measured. This is done with the focus on efficiency and productivity of the architecture when executing a real-world, non-optimized application as it is done in production runs. Therefore, the measured performance is the most realistic and most important one for the user since it governs the daily work, but is ignored by many benchmark suites. To cover this segment within IPACS, special benchmark cases have been developed for common simulation packages. These benchmarks are dimensioned and generated locally, depending on the number of processors, to achieve flexibility and scalability. The applications supported up to now in this way are FLUENT, STARCD and POWERFLOW.

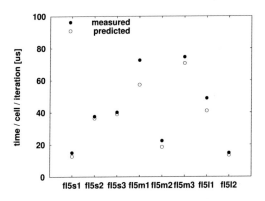

Figure 3.10: Measured execution time per cell and iteration (solid circles) compared to the predicted execution time (open circles) on an IBM pSeries 690 (1.3 GHz).

The knowledge of the performance data on all levels of the benchmark pyramid already allows inference and conclusion of strengths and weaknesses of a specific system and the influence on application specific performance. But in addition to that, performance modeling and prediction methods based on this data are developed, as shown on the right side of figure 3.7, which is described in the next chapter.

3.2.5 Grid Benchmarks

Grid computing is a vastly developing area in the field of HPC. There are several projects and initiatives like D-Grid [30], EGGE [31] or TeraGrid [32], just to name a few that are addressing the development, utilization and standardization of service grid infrastructures. Enterprise grids are gaining more and more attention and importance. With this the benchmarking and performance evaluation of grids becomes indispensable. Thereto, in addition to the benchmarks mentioned in the previous sections, specific grid benchmarks are provided within the IPACS project.

But providing grid benchmarks also implies the realization of a framework for the definition and execution of grid-adaptive applications. Therefore, an environment for connecting to and addressing of grid information systems, for the execution of benchmarks and the collection of results has been developed. Implemented as a web application and a web service, this environment enables the user to access grid services easily. This abstraction has also been chosen, since the standardization in grid computing still is in progress. In this way, interfaces to new and additional services and protocols can be easily added.

On the one hand, this framework is used to execute the benchmarks described above on grid resources. But on the other hand, specific grid benchmarks are provided. These benchmarks have been chosen to simulate typical work and data flows of a grid application.

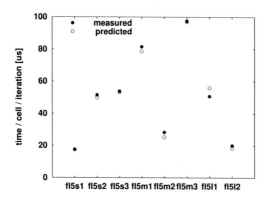

Figure 3.11: Measured execution time per cell and iteration (solid circles) compared to the predicted execution time (open circles) on an Alpha ES45 (1.0 GHz).

A detailed description is given in section 4.5, but a modular architecture of the program has been realized in order to allow for an easy update and extension to other benchmark probes if required by the development in grid computing.

3.3   Performance Modeling and Prediction Methods

Another main focus of the IPACS project is the development of methods for modeling and prediction of performance of commercial codes. The need for and the benefit of performance prediction techniques can be roughly divided into two areas: On the one hand, there is software development, where the understanding of the performance of an implemented algorithm is important for the developer in order to find and perhaps cure the bottlenecks of the code. For this aim, very precise modeling techniques are necessary, and detailed information and data from hardware counters and/or source code analysis is mandatory. But in many situations and on many systems, such a kind of information is hard or even impossible (e.g. for commercial software) to gain. On the other hand, performance prediction is also important for the user who wants to find out which hardware upgrade would improve the run-time of 'his' application most effectively. In this case, the data the modeling is based on must be easily obtainable, while an accuracy of $\approx 10\%$ for the prediction might be sufficient. But a reasonable estimate for the performance of an architecture, which cannot be accessed or is not even built yet, should be possible. This is the area that will be addressed by the modeling methods in this project.

Part II

Results Achieved by Each Project Partner

Chapter 4

Fraunhofer Institute for Industrial Mathematics (ITWM)

4.1 Low-Level Benchmarks

Low-level benchmarks for the measurement of memory and network performance have become well-known and have an established methodology. In addition to that, there is an existing pool of results for these benchmarks. For these reasons, we have chosen to base the IPACS low-level benchmarks upon the following software packages.

4.1.1 Memory Benchmark CACHEBENCH

The CACHEBENCH memory benchmark has been integrated from the open source benchmark suite LLCBENCH, which has been written by Philip J. Mucci. The benchmark is suitable to evaluate all possible memory hierarchies. It is thus especially interesting and useful for cache-based architectures. It is designed to determine the raw bandwidth for large, unit stride floating point memory operations.

Five different operations are implemented, three of them in two optimization levels, leading to eight different benchmarks. Each of them performs repeated access to data items in vectors of varying lengths. The accesses are repeated for a fixed amount of time, which is tunable at run-time. The performed operations are read, write, read/modify/write, memset and memcpy. The first three operations are implemented in a simple loop, which can be optimized by the compiler. A "hand-tuned" version has been implemented, in which a degree eight loop unrolling is implemented by hand. The comparison of the results for the different versions thus gives an estimate for the ability of the compiler in order to optimize the respective parts of code. In addition to that, there are implementations using the C library functions memset and memcpy. For a more detailed description of these benchmarks, we will refer to "The CACHEBENCH Report".

The memory benchmark from the existing package has been modified. It has been extensively used in order to analyze different architectures as well as different compilers. In these investigations, an incorrect behavior of the hand-tuned read benchmark under aggressive compiler optimization, which has been demonstrated in Figure 4.1, could be determined and fixed.

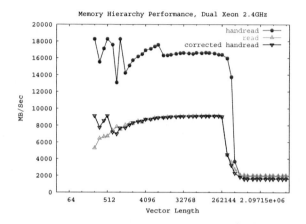

Figure 4.1: Performance results of the hand-tuned read benchmark with and without modification due to aggressive compiler optimization in comparison with the un-tuned read benchmark. The results have been measured on an Intel Dual Xeon node with 2.4 GHz using the Intel compiler with -O3 -unrolling.

The graph shows that the performance of the original version of the hand-read benchmark is twice as high as the un-tuned version. The reason is, that only half of the read accesses are actually performed. With the corrected version the two results coincide, as should be expected for a highly optimizing compiler. The necessary modifications have also been integrated in the LLCBENCH compiler suite.

With this improved version of CACHEBENCH, cross-platform and cross-compiler comparisons turn out to be very reliable. An example is given in Figure 4.2. Here, the results of the hand-tuned and read benchmarks on a Dual Opteron and a Dual Xeon node – with one and two benchmark instances running on the node at the same time – are compared. The most striking feature of this figure, besides the higher overall performance on the Opteron, is the difference between the single run and the two instance run for high vector lengths, i.e. for vector length which measure main memory accesses. Since on the Xeon architecture, the two processors share the bus to main memory, the bandwidth in is almost halved when two instances of the benchmark have to access the memory at the same time. In contrast to that, both of the two opteron processors have direct access to main memory due to AMD's HyperTransport technology (cc-numa). This results in an almost identical bandwidth for both benchmark instances, as can be seen in Figure 4.2.

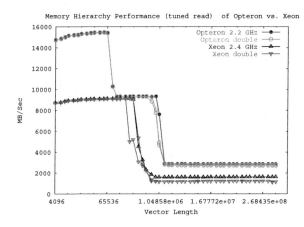

Figure 4.2: Performance results of the hand-tuned read benchmark on an Opteron and Xeon Dual node with one and two benchmarks running on the node. The pathscale and the Intel compiler has been used, respectively.

4.2 Network Benchmarks PMB and B$_{eff}$

The network benchmarks are based on the Pallas MPI Benchmarks (PMB)[1]. From this suite, Pallas – as a former partner of the IPACS project – has built an expressive selection in order to measure the latency and bandwidth of different communication patterns.

The suite incorporates four different benchmarks, two for point-to-point communication and two for collective communication. The former are PINGPONGand SENDRECV, which can be executed for two processes only or in a 'multi'–mode, where several pairs of processors communicate independently at the same time. The latter are BCASTand ALLREDUCE, i.e. a one-to-all and an all-to-all communication pattern. All these benchmarks operate on a data vector of increasing size to communicate, starting with a zero byte message to measure the pure latency of the network. Example results obtained for Infiniband, Myrinet and Quadrics with the PINGPONG benchmark are shown in Figure 4.3.

The resulting latency for zero byte messages and maximum bandwidth extracted from these measurements are

	Quadrics	Infiniband	Myrinet
latency [μs]	2.14	5.66	11.08
bandwidth [MB/s]	850	650	230

[1]Since September 2003, this benchmark suite is developed and distributed by Intel as Intel MPI Benchmarks (IMB).

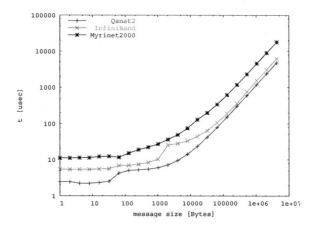

Figure 4.3: Network performance measured by the PMB PINGPONG benchmark on Infiniband, Myrinet2000 and Quadrics Qsnet2 interconnection.

Figure 4.3 also reveals the discontinuities in the performance, if the internal network protocol is changed upon reaching a specific message size. The discontinuity is especially distinct for Infiniband and Myrinet. This clearly demonstrates that low-level benchmarks not only measure the performance of the hardware, but also the effect of the corresponding drivers, settings and environments.

Originating as a spin-off from PMB the "effective Bandwidth" benchmark B_{eff} has been completely re-designed by the High Performance Computing Center Stuttgart (HLRS). In this benchmark the average of the performance of several communication patterns, topologies and message sizes is build. The topologies are build as ring and random distributions. All these patterns are implemented in three different ways: as SendRecv, Alltoallv and as non-blocking ISend and IRecv, from which the maximum performance is used. The averaging process weights small and large message in a different way to take into account that these are transferred with different bandwidth values in real applications. The final bandwidth number can be seen as an effective metric for a whole network performance. Some example results are shown in Tab. 4.1.

4.3   Open Source Application Benchmarks

One of the main focus points of the IPACS project has been the development of open source application benchmarks that reflect the performance of complex and realistic software projects. Two of these benchmarks are contributed by the ITWM. The full applications, on which the benchmarks are based, are still actively developed and used. These two benchmarks will be described in the following sections.

4.3.1 PARPACBENCH

The application benchmark PARPACBENCH has been extracted from the real production fluid dynamics code PARPAC. This code is a fluid dynamics code for three dimensional incompressible flows, which is based on the generalized lattice Boltzmann method. The basic idea of this approach is describing the Navier–Stokes equations by simulating simplified particle dynamics. In this formulation, arbitrary complex structures can be treated in a generic way.

The code has been developed by the ITWM and used for many internal and industrial projects. It accounts for a large range of fluid dynamical problems like stationary and transient flows, multi-phase flows, free surfaces or non Newtonian fluids in two and three dimensions. It thus is a good representation of a 'real', up-to-date fluid dynamics application.

The code is implemented in C++ using object-oriented design patterns. It is very efficiently parallelized by an automatic domain decomposition on the basis of load balance units of constant size. The graph and mesh partitioning library METIS is used for this decomposition. The inter-process communication is based on MPI. The communication structure is optimized by a graph-coloring algorithm in order to minimize the number of communication steps, making it a very effective parallel application.

From this code, a benchmark variant has been extracted. The main challenge in doing something like that is formulating a problem and extract a part of the code that is simple enough to be executed as a benchmark but not oversimplified and still characteristic for the full application. In addition to that, a scalable benchmark had to be created, which in particular implies that the geometry has to be scalable.

In order to address these problems, the calculation of the flow resistance of a complex porous geometry under an external pressure gradient has been chosen. The geometry is given by a cube with a generic internal structure as shown in Figure 4.4. The structure is generated internally by the benchmark itself and thus easily scales with the number of processors. In addition to that, no input data in the form of a geometry description or a separated pre-processing step is necessary. The benchmark can be run as a stand-alone application. The flow through this structure is simulated for a fixed number of time steps.

	2	4	8	16	32	64	128	256
Myrinet	53	53	51	48	45	42	39	34
Quadrics	87	87	84	82	78	76	72	64
IBM Colony SP Switch				39	30	24	19	17

Table 4.1: Benchmark results of B_{eff} for different network architectures, shown against the number of processors. The results are given in given in MB/s.

There are two performance metrics – in addition to the total run-time of the flow simulation – for this benchmark, which are derived from its output.

- The number of floating point operations per second (Flops). This number is calculated internally since the theoretical number of floating point operations for each calculation step is known. The number might vary slightly from the actual number reported via hardware counters, since e.g. optimization strategies of the compiler – which can lead to a different number of floating point operations – are not taken into account here. The number thus increases the comparability between different compilers, optimization levels and architectures.

- The number of discretization point updates per second. This should help with extrapolating the elapsed time for problems of different size. Moreover it should allow a rough comparison between different algorithms.

These efforts have resulted in a highly scalable benchmark. Results for one as well as for a few thousand processors have been generated, as is shown in Figure 4.5. The benchmark has been ported to a great variety of architectures and compilers. It runs under Linux, Windows and AIX on Intel, Opteron and IBM Power architectures. It has been compiled with gnu, Intel pathscale, visual age or pgi compilers. With the results obtained so far the high portability of the code has been demonstrated.

A collection of performance results for a variety of architectures and compilers is shown in Figs. 4.5-4.9. In general, a good scaling behavior is observed, even over two and three degrees of magnitude with respect to the number of processors and a corresponding increase in the size of the problem. The results for the parallel efficiency and the fraction of the theoretical peak performance are summarized in Tab. 4.2. These numbers demonstrate the well-known fact, that, for modern architectures and complex applications only a fraction of about $\approx 5\%$ of the theoretical peak performance can be reached.

	Intel Xeon, Myrinet	AMD Opteron, Infiniband	IBM SP RS6000	IBM pSeries Regatta	BlueGene/L
Parallel Efficiency	74.8%	82.9%	74.6%	71.4%	85.5%
Ratio Peak Performance	3.6%	11.1%	5.3%	3.0%	4.4%

Table 4.2: The parallel efficiency and the fraction of the theoretical peak performance for PARPACBENCH that are achieved for the highest number of processors shown in the corresponding figures.

4.3.2 DDFEM

In contrast to PARPACBENCH, the finite element code DDFEM has been developed from scratch to generate a finite element structural mechanics benchmark. Starting from the first benchmark version in 2002 it has grown to an efficient, powerful application that can be used for internal and external projects. DDFEM is a fully parallel finite element code for three-dimensional elasticity problems. It calculates the deformations and stresses within an elastic body under given external forces. It works on tetrahedral meshes, which are generated by the built-in mesh generator.

The code is implemented in C++ using object-oriented design patterns. The mesh partitioning is performed using the partitioning library METIS. The inter-process communication is based on MPI. The resulting large-size linear system of equation is solved iteratively in parallel using the PETSc library.

In order to use this code as a benchmark, a special benchmark problem had to be created with identical objectives to the ones described in section 4.3.1. Especially the scalability of the problem had to be taken into account. To this end, a generic structure – consisting of layers of solid cylinders, which are placed into an imaginary unit cube, (Figure 4.10) – has to be generated. The number and size of cylinders and layers are adjusted to the number of processors, leading to a constant load. The deformation of this structure under a constant normal external force then is calculated.

The main performance metric for this benchmark is the number of floating point operations, which is reported by the PETSc library for the iterative solution of the linear system of equations. This includes the mesh-generation state, which is not calculation-intense, but nevertheless an important part of the finite element method.

A collection of performance results is shown in Figs. 4.11-4.14. In general a good scaling behavior is observed. Especially for high number of processors a nice speed-up can be measured, see Figure 4.11. The good parallel efficiency from these results is summarized in Tab. 4.3. With respect to the slightly smaller absolute performance in comparison to PARPACBENCH ,it must be taken into account that the mesh-generation step is included.

	Intel Xeon, Myrinet	AMD Opteron, Infiniband	IBM SP RS6000	IBM pSeries Regatta
Parallel Efficiency	50.6%	87.4%	67.8%	82.2%

Table 4.3: The parallel efficiency and the fraction of the theoretical peak performance for DDFEM which are achieved for the highest number of processors shown in the corresponding figures.

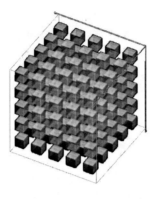

Figure 4.4: The generic cubic structure that is generated as a benchmark geometry for PARPACBENCH.

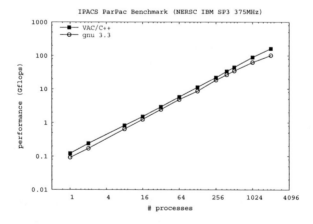

Figure 4.5: Performance measured by PARPACBENCH in GFlops on an IBM Power3+ System. The VAC/C++ compiler has been used.

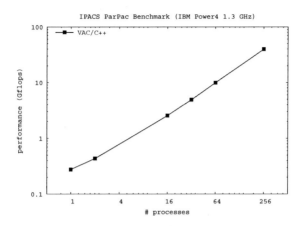

Figure 4.6: Performance measured by PARPACBENCH in GFlops on an IBM Power4 System. The VAC/C++ compiler has been used.

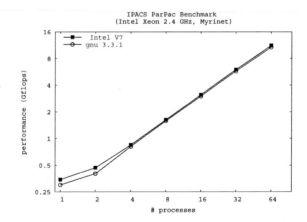

Figure 4.7: Performance measured by PARPACBENCH on an Intel Dual Xeon Cluster with Myrinet interconnection. The Intel compiler has been used.

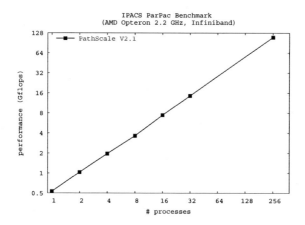

Figure 4.8: Performance measured by PARPACBENCH on an AMD Dual Opteron Cluster with Infiniband interconnection. The Pathscale compiler has been used.

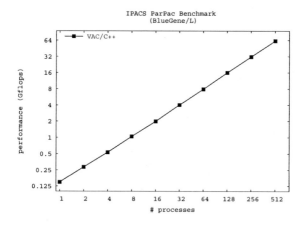

Figure 4.9: Performance measured by PARPACBENCH on an IBM BlueGene/L system. The VAC/C++ has been used.

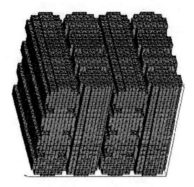

Figure 4.10: The generic structure of layers of cylinders which is generated as a benchmark geometry for DDFEM.

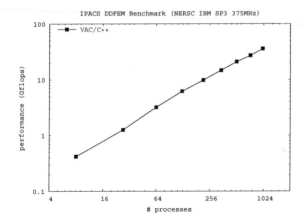

Figure 4.11: Performance measured by DDFEM in GFlops on an IBM Power3+ System. The VAC/C++ compiler has been used.

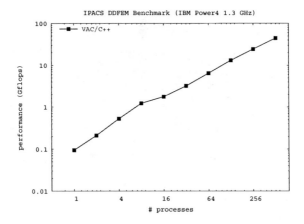

Figure 4.12: Performance measured by DDFEM in GFlops on an IBM Power4 System. The VAC/C++ compiler has been used.

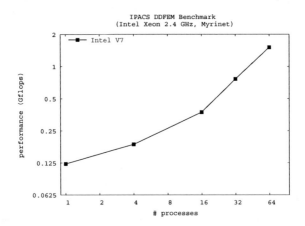

Figure 4.13: Performance measured by DDFEM on an Intel Dual Xeon Cluster with Myrinet interconnection. The Intel compiler has been used.

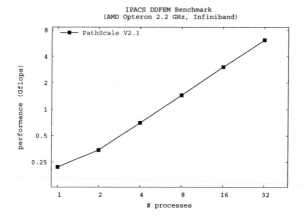

Figure 4.14: Performance measured by DDFEM on an AMD Dual Opteron Cluster with Infiniband interconnection. The Pathscale compiler has been used.

4.4 Commercial Applications

In addition to the open source application benchmarks described in section 4.3, a collection of benchmark cases for commercial applications has been developed by the ITWM. The applications that are supported in this way are

- Fluent, one of the world leading CFD codes, offers a solver for complex flow problems ranging from incompressible to highly compressible flows based on the finite volume approach. A wide variety of physical modeling and multiphysics for heat transfer, chemical reactions, multiphase flows, and other phenomena capabilities are available.

- STAR-CD, CD-adapco's technology leading CFD code, provides one of the most effective numerical methodologies for the simulation of steady and transient, laminar Newtonian and non- Newtonian flows. It offers a rich source of models for turbulence, combustion, radiation and multiphase physics on complex unstructured grids.

- POWERFLOW is a fluid flow simulation software for complex flow problems, that is based on Exa's patented DIGITAL PHYSICS technology, which is derived from the Lattice-Boltzmann Method. Its capabilities include internal and external flow simulations, turbulent boundary layer simulation, fluid mixing, aerodynamics and -acoustics.

For Fluent and Star-CD, a suite of benchmarks has been provided by the software vendor. These suites consist of a selection of industrial CFD applications of different size. They have been selected as representatives of the overall performance of the flow simulation. Since we are interested in a scalable benchmark, we cannot use a predefined problem case of constant size. Instead, a case based on a scalable geometry has to be generated. This means that, besides the geometry file, also the solver steering file, which describes the boundary conditions, defines inlet and outlet and controls the partitioning has to be adapted. Since it is not feasible to store and provide these kind of files – which may become quite huge – for any reasonable number of processors, they have to be generated locally.

The execution of these benchmarks thus has to be done in two steps: Firstly, the benchmark case has to be generated. The 'benchmark' hence mainly consists of a program, which creates the geometry file and the solver steering file. Especially, the latter strongly depends on the application, since it has to use its scripting language, its numbering scheme for the discretization entities, etc. For STARCD and POWERFLOW, in addition to that, the application specific pre-processor has to be invoked in order to create a problem description file suitable for a parallel run. The whole process is controlled by a script, which is started by the user. In a second step, the application is started with these generated files as input. An additional advantage of this separation of the process

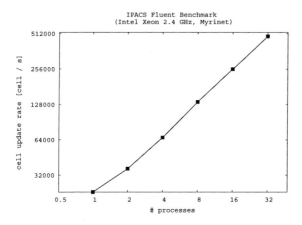

Figure 4.15: Performance results for Fluent measured with the IPACS Benchmark case.

into problem generation and execution as two different steps is that the generation, which might become memory-extensive, can be performed on a different system. It is therefore possible to chose the systems, which are suited for these steps independently with the control over e.g. the partitioning variables still available.

The benchmark case, which is generated, is similar to the one described in section 4.3.1 for PARPACBENCH: A cube with a generic internal structure is generated and the internal flow under an external pressure gradient is simulated. It has to be stressed that the results for different applications cannot be compared directly: slight modifications of the problem due to strengths and weaknesses of different solution methods have to be taken into account. The cases might differ in the distance to the boundary, the periodicity of the boundaries or in the size of the pressure gradient and the initial velocity. For the interested user the corresponding extensive information is provided in the control output of the generating scripts and of the benchmark runs.

The main performance metric for these benchmarks is the number of discretization cells/points/voxels updated per second. In contrast to the wall-time, from which it is derived, it allows for a direct comparison of runs with different problem size, i.e. different number of processors. The flop rate, on the other hand, is in general difficult to determine for a commercial application, since e.g. access to hardware counters can not be taken for granted on any architecture. Additionally the cell rate defined above is more important to the user, since the number of floating point operations might vary between different architectures or different software versions due to different optimizations or different algorithms.

Results for FLUENT, STARCD and POWERFLOW are shown in Figs. 4.15, 4.16 and 4.17, respectively. As can be seen in these figures, in general, a very good scaling behavior of the benchmarks can be observed. The resulting numbers for parallel efficiency are given

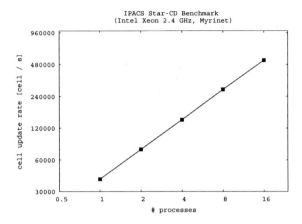

Figure 4.16: Performance results for Star-CD measured with the IPACS Benchmark case..

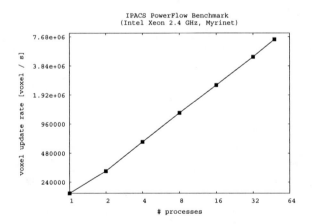

Figure 4.17: Performance results for POWERFLOW measured with the IPACS Benchmark case..

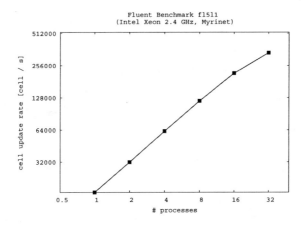

Figure 4.18: Performance results for Fluent measured with the fl5l1 Benchmark case taken from the Fluent benchmark suite.

	FLUENT	STARCD	POWERFLOW
Parallel Efficiency	65.9%	83.8%	82.0%

Table 4.4: The parallel efficiency of FLUENT, STARCD and POWERFLOW on the IPACS benchmarks, that are achieved for the highest number of processors shown in the corresponding figures.

in Tab. 4.4. For the purpose of a comparison, the results of a benchmark provided in the vendor benchmark suite mentioned above are shown in Figure 4.18. These results exhibit a similar performance and a similar speed-up behavior as the IPACS benchmark. The IPACS Benchmarks thus provides a number of scalable benchmarks for commercial software packages, which produce indeed characterizing performance data.

4.5 Grid-Benchmarks

A framework for the evaluation of the performance of grid components and grid services has been devolved. This includes not only the development of grid benchmarks but also the realization of an environment for the connection and addressing of grid information services, the execution of benchmarks and the collection of results. For this purpose a web service and a convenient user interface has been developed. From the user's point of view, the benchmarking process works in the following way: The user has to register and to log in through a web form, where he also has to specify the grid that he wants to be benchmarked and where he has access. In a next step, the benchmarks can be

Figure 4.19: Work and data flow of the 3-Node probe of the grid benchmarks..

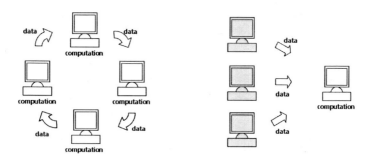

Figure 4.20: Work and data flow of the Circle (left) and Gather(right) probe of the grid benchmarks..

selected. Besides the cluster benchmarks described in the previous sections, three kind of grid probes, which have been proposed in [33], are integrated. These probes have been chosen to simulate typical work flows of a grid application

- A 3-Node probe, where data is sent from a first node to a second node. On this second node, some computations are performed on the data. Finally, the results are sent to a third node.

- A Circle probe, where each of a selected number of nodes – being arranged in a logical circle – receives data from its predecessor, performs some operation on the data and sends the results to its successor.

- A Gather probe, where data from a selected number of nodes is gathered by a central node in order to perform some operations on this data.

The main weight of these probes lies on the data transport and data flow that is critical for any grid application. This data flow is represented graphically in Figs. 4.19, 4.20. Additional probes can be added very easily, since the implementation is kept in a modular form.

After selecting the benchmarks, the user can specify options for the execution, i.e. the number of repetitions and in particular the daytime for the execution. It should be kept in mind that a grid, in contrast to a cluster, is an open system, which in general cannot be reserved for benchmarking purposes – it is always under load. Actually, the performance under load is an interesting benchmark result. Since this can vary significantly with the time of day, the option can be specified for the execution.

Finally, the user starts the benchmarks. With this, the web service will perform all the following steps, will transport the necessary data to the grid(-nodes), start the execution, monitors the progress and collect the results. This process can be monitored by the user, but no interaction is necessary. Finally, the results will be displayed. Besides the execution time as the main benchmark metric, details on the performance of the different steps of each probe will be provided. They can be investigated for a detailed analysis. The performance results can also be displayed graphically in comparison with previous executions in order to study the progression of performance with day-time, configuration changes, etc.

The benchmarking environment relies on the WS-resource framework of the Globus toolkit as the most advanced and most commonly used open source grid building systems and can easily be extended to additional standards like GLite or Unicore. It therefore provides a future-proof framework for the execution of benchmark in the fast changing area of grid computing.

4.6 Performance Prediction Methods

Another main focus of the IPACS project is the development of methods for performance modeling and prediction. Having the user of a software package in mind rather than the developer, these techniques should be simple and self-contained. Moreover they have to be based on data which can be obtained easily, i.e. benchmark data, simple run-time measurements and information provided by the application itself. On the other hand, an accuracy of $\approx 10\%$ is considered as sufficient. In the following sections we will describe several prediction methods for serial and parallel performance. All of those methods have been developed at the ITWM.

4.6.1 Serial Performance

In order to find a simplified approach to describe performance, some basic assumptions and conditions are necessary. For the class of CFD software considered here it is assumed that the main computational part of these programs provides a distinctive structure: It consists of a loop over elementary building blocks of the inspected geometry like points or cells. The memory size of such a cell is small enough (a few 100 Byte) to fit into L1 cache. The total amount for all cells on the other hand is too large to fit into L2 cache so that there is no cache reuse between different loops. The run-time then should mainly be given by the number of L1 cache hits and L2 cache misses as well as the associated bandwidths of the architecture. The memory bandwidths are measured by

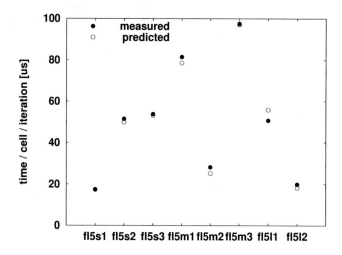

Figure 4.21: Measured execution time per cell and iteration (solid circles) compared to the predicted execution time (open circles) on an Alpha ES45 (1.0 GHz).

using CACHEBENCH(see section 4.1.1). These assumptions have been be shown to be met by e.g. the PARPACBENCHcode with the help of hardware counters.

In order to apply this model to commercial applications, where an instrumentation in general is not possible, the number of cache misses and memory references had to be determined approximately on a dual node system with a shared bus architecture – like the Intel Xeon [34]. In this system, the two processors posses their own cache hierarchy while the front-side bus for main memory accesses is shared. For the parallel execution of two independent processes with concurrent main memory accesses, this results in a reduced bandwidth as shown in [35] for different computational kernels. This behavior is triggered by running the application in parallel with an instance of CACHEBENCHon the second node which saturates the bus. From the reduced memory bandwidth the number of cache misses and memory references can be extracted.

This procedure has been applied to FLUENT using the benchmark cases, which are provided for this application by the vendor – together with performance results from different architectures [36]. Measuring and fixing the characteristic data for this application – as described above – has been done on an Intel Xeon. Together with available measurements of the memory system performance from CACHEBENCHand the theoretical peak flop rate we will obtain the results shown in figure 4.21 for an Alpha ES45 (1 GHz) for 8 different benchmark example cases.

As it can be seen, the prediction of the run-time works quite exact. The deviations are usually less then 10%. This simple approach thus seems to describe the main aspects of the application concerning the execution time reasonably well.

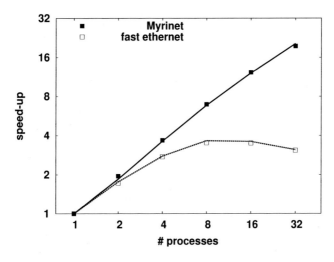

Figure 4.22: Measured speed-up compared to the prediction for FLUENT (case fl5m2) on an Intel Xeon (2.4 GHz) cluster using Myrinet (solid) and fast ethernet (open).

4.6.2   Parallel Performance

In order to capture the parallel performance and speed-up, a description of the communication pattern is necessary. The information mandatory to do this is the amount of transferred data, a description of the partitioning via the number of neighbors a processor has to communicate with and a characterization of the network performance. The first part is often reported by the application itself in order to estimate the quality of the applied partitioning. The network characteristics, bandwidth and latency, can be measured with PMB(see section 4.2). Assuming an optimal, well balanced inter-processor communication with a minimal number of communication steps, the time overhead for communication then can be calculated.

This has been applied to Fluent with an example benchmark case of medium size (fl5m2, 250000 cells, segregated implicit) on an Intel Xeon (2.4 GHz) cluster. To stress the influence of the interconnection, results with Myrinet and fast ethernet are shown in Figure 4.22. The measured speed-up is compared to the prediction. As it can be seen, the agreement is quite good and the necessary precision can be achieved.

Of course, such a simple description cannot account for more complicated structures like cache anomalies or competition for bandwidth. But the main characteristics seem to be described and – in connection with the model for single cpu performance – an extension with regard to cache usage is possible.

4.7 Instrumentation

For the collection of performance analysis information, a variety of tools is available, from profiling information generated by compiler flags (gprof), over special tracing versions of communication libraries (mpe) up to detailed hardware counter information through instrumented software. The availability and the access to such tools is strongly hardware- and software specific and it also depends on the configuration of the architectural environment. We note that the instrumentation of the applications and libraries in general cannot be done without modification of the code. In order to standardize this procedure, a generic instrumentation library and interface has been developed. The main idea is separating the instrumentation of the code from the calling sequence to a specific analyzing tool. This is achieved by an intermediate library, which provides generic calls for starting and stoping a tracing routine. These calls are inserted in the code into the segment under consideration. A corresponding C++ code segment is would be given by:

```
// Initialization of the Instrumentation Object
   Instrumentation Inst;
   ...
   Inst.start_tracing(CALCULATION);
   ... // code segment to be traced
   Inst.stop_tracing(CALCULATION);
```

The specific implementation of the `start_tracing` and `stop_tracing` calls for a given tool is provided by a corresponding library. In this way, the code has to be instrumented only once, and the decision, which tool will be used depending on the environment and on the desired information, can be made in the linking step by choosing the 'correct' library and without recompiling the whole code.

Implementations of this instrumentation library are provided for the mpi-tracing library *mpe*, for vampirtrace, for the hardware-counter library *papi* and for the IBM performance counter library *hpm*. The benchmarks of the IPACS benchmark suite are instrumented in an appropriate way. This simplifies the creation of e.g a detailed communication graph as shown in Figure 4.23 by using mpe enormously. The information is the basis for a detailed performance analysis and will support the user in the process of finding weaknesses and bottlenecks in his architecture.

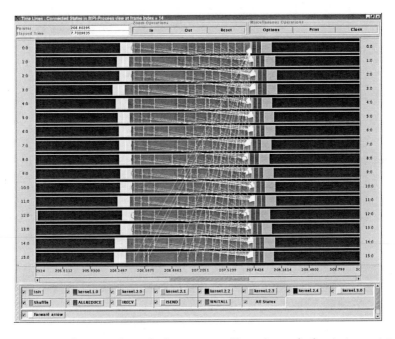

Figure 4.23: A screenshot of the mpe profiling data of the instrumentated TauBench code, visualized with jumpshot.

Chapter 5

University of Mannheim, IT Center

The University of Mannheim's IT-Center is responsible for the IPACS Software Architecture including the IPACS Repository, Web-Server, the IPACS Client and Execution Framework. The following subsections will describe the overall architecture and the interaction of these components starting from the user's perspective.

5.1 IPACS Environment – User's Benefits and Requirements

Besides the benefits for benchmark practioniers and scientists provided by the IPACS benchmark suite, we had the goal of generating more benefits through further (software) tools, components and consulting activities. The consulting activities were understood as high-level analysis, forecasting, budgeting and procurement advice. These activities were aimed to be carried out by each project partner during the project founding time and also after it in order to generate some revenue to be able to continue IPACS for some time without further founding. In order to provide high quality consulting advice, we needed a firm, reliable, well-structured and up-to-date data basis of systems and benchmarks. In order to develop and maintain such a strong data basis, we have chosen to open the data basis to the benchmarking community and provide everybody also with aids to make optimal use of it. This should create sufficient incentives for the community to supply benchmarking results to the data basis.

So to generate benefits for the benchmarking community we discussed several use case scenarios. We identified the following groups as potential users:

- The overall group is naturally centered around HPC sites at research, government and companies, which can be both HPC system vendors and appliers of HPC systems in various industry segments.

- The HPC group does however not only consist of the persons at a site running a system in the TOP500 list, but also contains every other person on smaller sites running at least some form of computing cluster for all imaginable purposes.

- People working for an HPC systems vendor or integrator.

In more detail, the groups consist of diverse people with roughly the following roles:

- Benchmarking employees, i.e. people which have to carry out benchmarks, at sites or vendors.

- Administrators of HPC systems, i.e. people which administer compute servers or install, maintain and deploy systems.

- Managers of HPC sites, i.e. people who plan, manage and purchase compute servers for their business uses.

- Analysts and controllers at HPC sites, these are people which make recommendations and check correct (financial) usage of HPC systems.

- Managers, marketing personnel and technicians of HPC vendors, i.e. people involved in designing, integrating, building and selling HPC systems.

From this overview of potential users we expect two main usage categories:

- *Information retrieval*, i.e. all kinds of questions about the (benchmarking) performance of certain systems, classes of systems, development over time, extrapolated trends, performance prediction for certain applications, discussion about results and insight in factors determining performance.

- *Execution support*, i.e. all kinds of help, guidance and support a novice and mature benchmarker would require to setup and run benchmarks and all kinds of help to assess the correctness and performance of certain systems. The last point could be ideally solved by a tight connection to the information retrieval component.

Information retrieval will be interesting to practically all potential users and execution support will be interesting mainly to benchmarkers, administrators and technicians.

For the design of an information retrieval component one can build on a well studied theoretical concept of information retrieval systems, so called business intelligence reference architecture. These systems consist mainly of the following building blocks [37] *Data integration* to collect data from external systems. In our case this means collecting benchmark results and system metadata from benchmark output produced on an HPC system. *Data management* consists of the repository database, database design and transport formats (e.g. XML DTDs). *Information delivery* describes the actual front end and its capabilities to users. In our case these could be all kinds of reporting tables and graphics, components for analytical processing (e.g. Kiviat diagrams for multidimensional assessment), data mining with customized queries and reports and collaboration support for commenting and result discussion. *Analytic applications* are in our case performance prediction for general systems or certain applications and planing and configuration tools.

For execution support, there is little known besides the classical configure, make and make install triade accompanied by readme files. From our experience, we know that many novice benchmarkers have trouble to run the Linpack benchmark, at least producing good results (i.e. high MFLOP rates). So our first goal must be to provide a mostly automated or interactive way to get the benchmarks executed. This is far more complicated as producing a single binary executable, it is hard to extract system metadata (e.g. CPU speed, cache size, interconnect speed, interconnect topology). Various batch systems and security constraints must be taken into account. Once a benchmark can be run automatically under the supervision of an IPACS component, we could provide many kinds of comparisons and analysis. E.g. one can directly compare the produced benchmark result to the results obtained on other systems by asking the information retrieval component. This directly leads to the identification of wrong software or hardware configurations and hardware bottlenecks (e.g. slow interconnection network). This information can also be very helpful to vendors in order to avoid customer complains. Having all these results and metadata available, it can be further used to come up with performance predictions for desired hardware configurations even for new, not jet available hardware.

In the following a tight connection between the two components could bring extra benefits. The execution support component can provide comparisons of other benchmarks and systems according to the current state of the benchmarking process. The information retrieval component can execute more precise queries based on the hard- and software characteristics determined in the execution component.

Now that we have identified benefits and requirements of potential users, we will turn to the design of appropriate software components in the next section.

5.2 The Software Architecture of the IPACS Environment

When faced with a decision to select an appropriate architectural design meeting the requirements stated in the last section, there are at least three main alternatives.

1. A *web-only system*, i.e. a central Web-server maintains all information and clients access it with a browser (using also down- and uploads).

2. A *totally distributed system*, i.e. the (downloaded) system is autonomous, contains its own repository, all benchmarks and tools, eventually sending results.

3. A *client - server system*, i.e. some part of the system resides on a central server (e.g. web-content, repository) and other parts being distributed (e.g. client, browser).

The first approach is the standard way, used e.g. by the TOP500 site and most other benchmarking sites. This design has the advantage, that everything is centralized and can efficiently maintained from one place. A disadvantage is that users can (only) retrieve and consume information and can't get support (other than explanations in the web) to run benchmarks on their own computers.

The second approach gives users complete control and support for running and evaluating benchmarks on their computers. Users can put results in the local repository for evaluation and nobody else will be able to see good or inferior results at this time. This feature was mandated by some users. However, the maintainers of the system have to develop the distributed system but would have no knowledge on what results are produced and eventually get published.

The third approach can keep important pieces in a central location, e.g. the repository with benchmark results and retrieval components, and can distribute parts which actively support the users in running the benchmarks. The distributed and central parts could be more or less integrated, i.e. allowing totally disconnected operation of the components or require some tight coupling and information exchange. Tight coupling has the advantage of removing data redundancy, but has the disadvantage in that HPC centers are sometimes closed shops with no online internet connection.

Taking these considerations into account, we decided to pursue the third approach (see also [38]). In summary it has the following advantages:

- It was the most flexible initial design, which was assumed to be adaptable to upcoming problems or to a shift of changes of overall project conceptions. It could have also evolved into the other two approaches, if required by some constraints.

- It gives us the chance of reaching and supporting users, which are only interested in online benchmark information retrieval (e.g. decisions for procurement).

- It will allow development of support tools and guidance of novice and mature users for the execution, tuning and evaluation of benchmarks.

- By a tight integration between the distributed client and the server, the benchmarking community can benefit from up-to-date and standardized benchmarks and up-to-date benchmark results in the repository.

- The benchmarkers will also get instant online comparisons and evaluations of the performed benchmark runs.

The tight integration of client and repository is also one of the major disadvantages of this design. Users (e.g. from HPC companies) may not be willing to disclose (eventually bad) benchmark results. Inferior results coming from either unexperienced benchmarkers, or not (yet) optimized hardware, undisclosed hardware, software problems (e.g. for large processor numbers) or simply by having to comply to some legal regulation or policy. As a remedy to this problem we have taken care that the client can also operate in an offline mode, where all support in executing and tuning of the benchmark is available. However, in this mode, no online evaluation and online performance prediction is available. Another remedy is that users are not required to provide us (and the community) with real user information and can use online evaluation in an anonymous way.

So in conclusion, the software architecture of the IPACS environment consists of three main components.

- A (so-called) *repository server*, which acts a central data store for all relevant benchmark information and all necessary information on the status of an ongoing benchmark run (configuration, compilation, execution, results).

- The *client and execution framework*, so called IPACS client, for the distributed support of benchmarkers.

- The *information retrieval component*, realized by a web server with various evaluation and comparison tables and graphics (also multi-dimensional Kiviat diagrams) together with components for performance prediction.

In the following (sub-)sections, we will discuss the three components, their respective duties, their design, their implementations and problems. Finally, we will discuss an evaluation of the usefulness of the design and the actual implementation from a user's perspective.

5.3   IPACS Repository

This section describes in-depth the essential design and implementation aspects of the IPACS repository server. It starts with an illustration of the thematic scope and explains the main background and objectives. Afterwards, the IPACS data model is introduced by an UML Class Model and Entity-Relationship Diagram. Finally, the IPACS repository server software architecture is presented including communication, business and persistence layer.

5.3.1   The Scope of the IPACS Repository

The purpose of the IPACS repository server is to act as single information source and data store for HPC information, benchmark results and benchmark files. For this purpose, the repository server has to manage details about registered high performance computers, e.g. site information, common computer details as well as technical parameters regarding to the hard- and software environment.

The repository server has to store all benchmark results for each HPC. In order to determine performance differences that may result from soft- and hardware updates in time, it becomes necessary to store several results of a specific benchmark type in a chronological order. Only the combination of a specific computer configuration (an HPC could have several computer configurations in time) together with a specific benchmark result enables a benchmarker to do an in-depth performance analysis e.g. in order to detect a bottleneck that may be a result of the current network infrastructure. Additionally, the repository server has to manage the relationship between benchmark results and different computer configurations. Moreover, the repository server also has to take into account that benchmarks could be executed on any arbitrary number of processors. Consequently, for every HPC the repository server has to deal with, benchmarks results of a specific benchmark type are corresponding to the two dimensions: time and number of processors.

To assist users in the selection and execution of appropriate benchmarks, the repository server has to handle all information about available IPACS benchmarks (sources and binaries). Together with the IPACS client, the repository server has to offer suitable benchmark files regarding to the current HPC configuration.

5.3.2   The IPACS Data Model

One design aspect of the benchmark repository was to define a unique data model that covers all real-world details or variations in High Performance Computing. Regarding to the objectives mentioned in chapter 5.3.1, the IPACS data model has to deal with at least five different categories of information:

- **Client:** Information about a real world IPACS client instance used by a benchmarker to execute benchmarks. This contains data like an IP-address of the computer on which the client is executed, a unique identification number (ID) and the date of the last usage.

- **Computer:** Represents general information aspects of a HPC, commonly static attributes like computer name, computer type, vendor or HPC architecture.

- **Computer Configuration:** Describes the dynamic part of a HPC like the current hard- and software environment, e.g. name and version of the operating system, CPU-type, current MPI-version, etc.

- **Site:** Represents information about the location and the maintainer of a HPC, e.g. including a URL of the department and/or a phone number.

- **Benchmark:** Represents a benchmark result for a specific benchmark type like serial disk I/O performance (MB/s) in case of PRIOMARK.

Figure 5.1 shows a slightly simplified UML class diagram with the five main components: client, computer, computer-configuration, benchmark and site. A client represents an abstraction of the real world benchmark client that could be connected to a computer. One computer is located at one site and associated with a current computer-configuration. Whereas a computer represents static attributes like computer type, date of installation and perhaps a date of shutdown, a computer-configuration instead covers dynamic attributes of a HPC like the current hard- and software environment (e.g. name and version of the operating system, current CPU-type or the current MPI-version). A benchmark

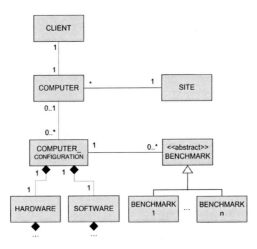

Figure 5.1: Simplified UML Class diagram describing a part of the data model.

represents a single benchmark result including characteristic values, an ASCII output of the benchmark run and maybe one ore more diagrams. For every benchmark as part of the IPACS benchmark suite, a benchmark subclass represents the specific measurement criteria of a specific benchmark like PMB or PARPACBENCH (in the diagram pictured as benchmark 1 - benchmark n). Every benchmark (result) is related to a particular computer configuration, and due to possible changes in the hard- and software environment in time, a computer could have several configurations and, with it, also different benchmark results - even for the same benchmark type. Other details like subclasses of hard- and software have been omitted in figure 5.1 for the sake of clarity.

Figure 5.2 graphically illustrates the conceptual structure of the computer-configuration of a HPC. As mentioned above, the computer-configuration contains hardware and software issues. The hardware consists of one interconnect and several equal or different nodes. Every node represents one or more CPUs, memory and caches. A configuration contains also some of the software equipment, in detail tools, compilers, cluster-software and an operating system.

As a rule, people who are interested in using the IPACS web-presentation and information retrieval component, want to compare different benchmark results in contrast with different HPCs. In order to satisfy this requirement adequately, the characteristic values of a benchmark result should be aggregated into a single table. Beyond that, the web-presentation and information retrieval component also have to provide a mechanism to sort these characteristic values. It turns out, that a relational database management system (RDBMS) could support the web-presentation regarding to these requirements best of all (for more details cf. to 5.3.3.3).

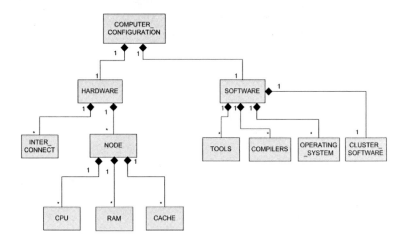

Figure 5.2: UML Class diagram describing the Hardware and Software-Configuration.

After deciding to use a relational database as backend, the UML class diagram has to be transformed into an entity relationship diagram. Figure 5.3 shows the simplified entity relationship diagram again with the five main components: client, computer, computer-configuration, benchmark and site. The complete entity relationship diagram is available in appendix C. Subsequently, a relational model was derived from the entity relationship diagram and the resulting tables are available in appendix D.

5.3.3 Architecture

Providing the ability to use the IPACS architecture from a wide variety of heterogeneous computer systems, we have made a decision to implement our architecture based on the platform-independent programming language Java. To realize a distributed client/server environment as suggested in section 5.2, several different scenarios have been seriously considered.

The development of enterprise applications in Java is commonly based on SUNs J2EE platform [39] either by using the widespread Enterprise Java Beans (EJB) component model [40] or by implementing the Java Servlet technology [41].

The EJB component model represents an architecture for the development and deployment of component-based and distributed business applications. It provides a framework architecture for building middleware components that are created, controlled, and destroyed by the J2EE container. The container frees the developer from having to deal with code that handles transactional behavior, security, connection pooling, or threading (*separation of concerns*).

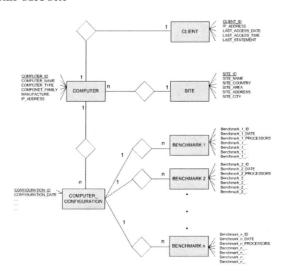

Figure 5.3: Simplified Entity Relationship Diagram.

At first glance, an Enterprise Java Beans approach might well be the solution of choice, since the specification ensures infrastructure services in an "out-of-the-box" fashion. However, due to the flaws of available open source implementations (e.g. memory leak in JBoss 2.x) at the time our project started in 2002, the EJB component model was quickly discarded.

Java Servlets as another part of the J2EE specification provide a component-based, platform-independent method for building web-based applications. Servlets are modules of Java code that run in a server application to answer client requests commonly by using HTTP. Servlets receive all the benefits of the mature Java language and have access to all J2SE APIs, including JDBC to access enterprise databases.

After discussing our overall purpose and the advantages and disadvantages of Java Servlets, we expect the following benefits for our project:

- Since Servlets provide easy to use methods for client communication over HTTP, this technology is best suited to the need of our communication model of the repository server and the IPACS client (See chapter 5.3.3.1).

- The Servlet container provides transaction management, which is indispensable in case of multiple clients who simultaneously access the repository server at the same time.

- Several free and stable open source implementations of Servlet-containers are available (e.g. Apache's Tomcat [42]).

The server-side software is divided into three layers, namely communication-, business and persistence layer. The following sections will describe these different layers separately.

5.3.3.1 Communication Layer

This section will introduce the communication layer and describes the communication protocol between the repository server and IPACS benchmark client.

In the client/server communication context, several message-oriented middleware standards like CORBA (Common Object Request Broker Architecture), RMI (Remote Method Invocation) or SOAP (Simple Object Access Protocol) have been considered. Although these approaches are based on higher-level protocols providing easier programming APIs, they all require a sophisticated infrastructure like setting up an Object Request Broker in case of CORBA. To ensure an easy deployment of the benchmark client in an unknown environment we decided to keep the software requirements as low as possible. Therefore, we stick to the well-known, robust and ubiquitous HTTP-protocol on port 80 in order to avoid problems with the infrastructure like firewalls (see also [38]).

As mentioned above, using a Servlet approach allows the developer to implement the domain-specific aspects exclusively while the technical concerns in particular low-level communication aspects are handled by the container. In this context, the Servlet container provides an interface to receive HTTP requests and generates a suitable response.

To realize the communication between IPACS benchmark client and repository server, we developed a communication protocol based on HTTP and XML-messages. Compared to other solutions, e.g. serialized objects or web-services, plain XML-messages lead to another advantage: In the unlikely case of firewall or network problems, the XML-files could also be transmitted with other services e.g. ftp or email.

Together with the IPACS benchmark experts, a global XML-structure based on a common Document Type Definition (DTD) file was developed. The IPACS-DTD specifies the handling of benchmark results, site information, computer information and computer configuration (cf. section 5.3.2). Even more, it describes the exchange of meta information between client and server. In this context, meta-information describes a set of data that is necessary to ensure the client/server communication, like IP-addresses or the currently used version of the benchmark client. The full IPACS-DTD is available in appendix B.

An IPACS-DTD conform XML-message is generally divided into two parts: A header for meta-information and a body that contains specific data. The first part contains meta-information like a unique client-ID or a statement that describes what the server (business_layer) should do with the data contained in the body. The `<ipacs_data>`-part could include a benchmark result, some information about a HPC or could even be empty.

The principles of the client/server communication sequence and the structure of the XML-messages will be briefly described by the following example: To initiate the benchmark process (for more information about the IPACS benchmark process cycle see 3.1.1), a client requests a list of available benchmarks, downloads the sources and starts the build

process e.g. by using the benchmark execution framework (cf. section 5.5.6). After the
benchmark run is complete, the client submits the results to the repository server and
displays the corresponding results.

```
<?xml version="1.0" encoding="iso-8859-1"?>
<!DOCTYPE ipacs SYSTEM "http://www.ipacs-benchmark.org/
        download/ipacs_dtd_01.dtd">
<ipacs>
  <ipacs_header>
        <statement>get available_benchmarks</statement>
        <client_id>3902</client_id>
        <client_version>1.0 RC_27</client_version>
  </ipacs_header>
  <ipacs_data/>
</ipacs>
```

Listing 5.1: client request: get available Benchmarks

Listing 5.1 shows a simple client request. In the <ipacs_header> the statement
get available_benchmarks requests a list of available IPACS benchmarks. The
<client_id>, 3902 in this case, represents a unique instance of an IPACS client.
This tag is necessary to enable the repository server to distinguish between requests
of different clients. Just the use of an IP-address for identification is not sufficient,
because a web-proxy could alter the original IP-address in a TCP/IP-package. The last
tag (<client_version>) shows the currently used client version, which is 1.0 release
candidate 27 in this case. This tag ensures the ongoing development of both, client and
repository server, even some older versions of the client are still in use.

Every communication sequence will be initiated by the IPACS benchmark client.
After checking the formal correctness of XML-messages regarding to the IPACS-DTD
(see appendix B) the server verifies the Client-ID as well as the IP-address. Subsequently,
the repository server updates some log-files, analyzes the <statement>-tag and passes
the data of the <ipacs_data> to a suitable subroutine. Afterwards, the repository server
generates an XML-based message as an answer that may confirm the client request or in
case of an exception includes an error message and a standardized error code (cf. section
5.3.3.2).

```
<?xml version="1.0" encoding="iso-8859-1"?>
<!DOCTYPE ipacs SYSTEM "http://www.ipacs-benchmark.org/
        download/ipacs_dtd_01.dtd">
<ipacs>
  <ipacs_header>
     <statement>send available_benchmarks</statement>
  </ipacs_header>
  <ipacs_data>
```

```xml
<available_benchmarks>
...
<benchmark>
<name>pmb</name>
    <version>2.2.1</version>
    <website>http://www.ipacs-benchmark.org/index.php?
        s=description&amp;bm=PMB</website>
    <directlyExecutable>true</directlyExecutable>
</benchmark>
...
<benchmark>
    <name>taubench</name>
    <version>1.1</version>
    <website>http://www.ipacs-benchmark.org/index.php?
        s=description&amp;bm=TAUBENCH</website>
    <directlyExecutable>true</directlyExecutable>
</benchmark>
</available_benchmarks>
</ipacs_data>
</ipacs>
```

Listing 5.2: server response: available Benchmarks

In the given example, the client requests a list of IPACS benchmarks including a download URL from the repository server. Listing 5.2 shows the corresponding server response. In the <ipacs_header>, neither an id nor a version tag is available, because the client does not have to distinguish between responses from different servers. The <statement>-tag states that the client's request was accepted and the <ipacs_data> contains a list of available benchmarks. Even if the simplified listing 5.2 includes only two <benchmark>-parts, the complete listing contains 11 benchmarks, namely B_{eff}, CACHEBENCH, DDFEM, FLUENT, LINPACK, PARPACBENCH, PMB, POWERFLOW, PRIOMARK, STARCD and TAUBENCH. For every benchmark, the name, the most recent version and an URL to an information web-site is available. Additionally, the tag <directlyExecutable> indicates, if a benchmark could be automatically compiled and executed by the benchmark execution framework (see section 5.5.6).

```xml
<?xml version="1.0" encoding="iso-8859-1"?>
<!DOCTYPE ipacs SYSTEM "http://www.ipacs-benchmark.org/
        download/ipacs_dtd_01.dtd">
<ipacs>
  <ipacs_header>
        <statement>get benchmark_url</statement>
        <client_id>3902</client_id>
        <client_version>1.0 RC_27</client_version>
```

```
</ipacs_header>
<ipacs_data>
  <benchmark_request>
    <benchmark_name>taubench</benchmark_name>
    <benchmark_version>1.0</benchmark_version>
    <benchmark_type>source</benchmark_type>
  </benchmark_request>
</ipacs_data>
</ipacs>
```

Listing 5.3: client request: getbenchmark_url

The next step from the client's point of view is to interact with the user in order to select one benchmark (cf. section 5.5.5.1). The client again, sends a request to the server in order to ask for the location of the selected benchmark (listing 5.3). In this example, the user has selected the TAUBENCH in version 1.0 (cf. section 6.1). The user has also decided to get a source version of the TAUBENCH benchmark. Depending on the current hard- and software environment of the HPC, sometimes binary versions of benchmarks are also available.

```
...
<ipacs_data>
  <benchmark_url>http://www.ipacs-benchmark.org/
      download/pmb/1.0/Linux/pmb_i686_Linux_2.4.20.tar.gz
  </benchmark_url>
</ipacs_data>
...
```

Listing 5.4: server response: send benchmark_url

The client receives the URL of the benchmark (listing 5.4) and initiates the download from the IPACS web-presentation. After a successful compilation and execution on the HPC, the client gathers the measurement results (cf. section 5.5.5.4) and submits it to the repository server.

Listing 5.5 shows the XML-message that represents a measurement result of TAUBENCH. The <ipacs_data> part contains first of all the name of the benchmark. To be able to use the same XML-structure for all benchmarks of the IPACS benchmark suite, it was necessary to divide benchmarks into further sub-benchmarks. E.g. PMB consists of four sub-benchmarks, namely ALLREDUCE, BCAST, SENDRECV and PINGPONG. It follows the number of processors on which the benchmark was executed. And again, to be able to use the same XML-structure for all benchmarks, benchmark specific values are encapsulated with the <characteristic_number> tag. In this example the TAUBENCH has three different values, which are floating point operation rate, the number of grid points and the communication ratio. For more details about these values cf. section 6.1.

```
...
<ipacs_data>
  <benchmark>
     <name>TAUBENCH</name>
     <sub_benchmark>
         <name>TAU</name>
         <processors>2</processors>
            <characteristic_number>
               <name>FLOATING_POINT_OPERATION_RATE</name>
               <value>29.247</value>
            </characteristic_number>
            <characteristic_number>
                <name>GRID_POINTS</name>
                <value>262144</value>
            </characteristic_number>
            <characteristic_number>
                <name>COMMUNICATION_RATIO</name>
                <value>0.001</value>
            </characteristic_number>
            <detailed_output>
            This is TauBench.
            Evaluating kernels - please be patient.

            - kernel_1_0 :    30.556 secs -   120.719 mflops
            - kernel_1_1 :    11.023 secs -    51.853 mflops
            - kernel_2_1 :    23.443 secs -   111.049 mflops
            - kernel_2_2 :   905.203 secs -     3.533 mflops
            - kernel_2_3 :     4.390 secs -   147.060 mflops
            - kernel_2_4 :   139.707 secs -    10.404 mflops
            - kernel_3_0 :    21.182 secs -   338.934 mflops

            total :   1134.821 secs -       29.247 mflops

               ...
            </detailed_output>
      </sub_benchmark>
   </benchmark>
</ipacs_data>
...
```

Listing 5.5: client request: submit result

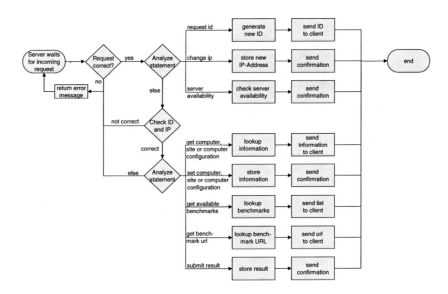

Figure 5.4: Communication Sequence between client and repository server.

5.3.3.2 Business Layer

After introducing the communication layer in the previous section, this section focuses on the business logic, including workflow management, image conversion service, error and exception handling.

Workflow Management

As previously noted, the repository server backend is based on the Java Servlet technology and a relational database (for details about the persistence layer see section 5.3.3.3). Based on a SuSE Linux Server, the following software is currently installed:

- MySQL-Database (Version Max-4.1.10a-3.4) with InnoDB-extension

- Servlet-Container: Jakarta-Tomcat (Version 5-5.0.30-4)

- Java: j2sdk (Version 1.4.2_08)

- Database-Driver: JDBC (`com.mysql.jdbc.Driver`, version 3.0.17)

In the Servlet-container, a Java-Servlet (`IPACSServer`) analyzes the XML message of incoming HTTP requests. Depending on the content of the `statement` in the `<ipacs_header>` (cf. section 5.3.3.1), the Servlet interacts with a variety of different Java objects and finally produces an XML message as a response for the client.

Figure 5.4 pictures the workflow of the repository server. The activated server waits for an incoming client request. When the server receives a request, it checks the formal correctness of XML-messages regarding to the IPACS-DTD (cf. appendix B) and in case of an invalid or not well-formed XML request, the server generates an error message. If the request is valid and well formed, the server analyzes the `statement` of the `<ipacs_header>`. If the statement equals `request id`, `change ip` or `server availability`, the repository server initiates the corresponding process without additional security checks and verifications.

The communication protocol as described in section 5.3.3.1 requires a unique identification number (ID) for every IPACS client. When a client establishes the first connection to the repository server, the client requests a unique ID by sending the `request id` statement to the server. The client stores the received ID and inserts it from now on in every communication message as part of the `<ipacs_header>`. The server on the other hand, stores the IP-address of the client for a later security check.

The second statement (`server availability`) is intended to detect potential server or network problems. Usually, when the Servlet engine and the database are available, the server sends a `true` as response back to the client. In the very unlikely case that the servlet engine or the database are not available, the connection to the server was refused and indicates some problems at the server-side.

The third statement (`change ip`) is essential to implement an efficient security-mechanism to prevent a hacker from gaining unauthorized access to the repository server. The IPACS engineers have decided not to use an encryption mechanism to give benchmarkers the possibility to track the complete client/server communication. The IPACS security mechanism instead is based on a complex client-ID and IP-address verification mechanism on the server-side. Even although this approach is probably not the securest solution, it prevents most cases of unauthorized access. Moreover, it allows benchmarkers to monitor the complete communication session. Before accepting a client statement the server checks if the stored IP-address is equal to the one of the current request. The mechanism causes two problems. First, a web-proxy could manipulate the IP-address in a TCP/IP-package and second, the client's IP-address could change in time.

To solve the first problem, the IPACS benchmark client adds an extra HTTP header field, that contains the local client IP-address. In detail, the client uses the `setRequestProperty` method for the `HttpURLConnection` to add a `client-ip` field. Even though this mechanism will solve the potential problem with a web-proxy, it is not sufficient to solve the second problem. In detail, an IP-address could have been changed when the IPACS client starts a second time, e.g. in case the computer obtains it's IP-address dynamically from a DHCP server. Therefore the client automatically detects if an IP-address has changed after a restart and sends a `change ip` request to the server, containing both, the old and the new IP-address. The server checks if the old IP-address equals the stored one in the database and updates the value accordingly.

For all statements excepting those already mentioned, the server starts the ID verification process before further proceeding. As described above, the server looks up the stored client's IP-address in the database for the given `<client_id>` as part of the `<ipacs_header>`. If the IP-address from the database equals the IP-address of the special HTTP header field `client-ip`, the server proceeds to pass the `<ipacs_data>`-part to an appropriate method. In any other case, the server denies further processing and sends an error-message "Security-Error: Incoming and stored IP-Address are different".

Command	Meaning
`request id`	First time, a client contacts the repository server to get an unique Client-ID.
`send computer`	The client sends information about the HPC to the server (such as name, type, architecture, etc.).
`get computer`	The client requests information about the HPC to the client (such as name, type, architecture, etc.).
`send computer_configuration`	The client sends detailed hardware and software information of the HPC to the server.
`get computer_configuration`	The client requests detailed hardware and software information of the HPC.
`send site`	The client sends the site information to the server.
`get site`	The client requests the site information from the server.
`get available_benchmarks`	The client requests a List with all available benchmarks.
`get benchmark_url`	The client requests the download URL of a particular benchmark.
`submit result`	The client sends a result of an already executed benchmark to the server.
`server availability`	Check, if the repository server works properly.
`change ip`	Replaces the registered IP-address of a client.

Table 5.1: Repository Server Statements

After the verification process is completed, the repository server updates some log-files e.g. to store the last statement including the current access time. Depending on the client request, the server

- looks up information of an HPC in the database and sends it to the client,

- stores information of an HPC in the database,

- composes a list of currently available benchmarks and sends it to the client,

- sends a benchmark URL for a selected benchmark to the client,

- or stores an incoming benchmark result in the database.

Table 5.1 gives a brief overview of all supported repository server statements. In case an error occurred, the server sends a detailed error or message including a unique error number to the client. For more information about the error and exception handling cf. section 5.3.3.2.

A potential sequence of client/server interaction could be as following:

1. A client contacts the server for the first time.

2. The server generates a unique ID and sends it to the client. Client and server store this ID.

3. In interaction with a user, the client requests a list of available IPACS benchmarks from the server.

4. Since there is no current HPC-Configuration available, the client determines the hardware and software-configuration on the high performance computer. Afterwards the client has to transmit it to the server.

5. The server analyzes the received computer configuration and sends a list with all benchmarks, which are executable on the HPC, back to the client.

6. A user selects one benchmark for execution.

7. The client asks the server for the download URL of the selected benchmark.

8. The server sends the download URL back to the client.

9. After download, compilation and execution of the benchmark on the HPC, the client sends the benchmark result to the server. The server stores this result in the database.

10. Within user interaction, the client could now continue with step 6 in order to select a further benchmark.

Image Conversion Service

As described in section 5.2, the web-presentation and information retrieval component is the entry point for people who are interested in benchmarking High Performance Computers. All information that could be viewed at the web-presentation will be provided by direct access to the MySQL database on the repository server (cf. section 5.4). Beside the aggregated and human readable benchmark results, the repository server also provides convenient diagrams. Whereas some diagram types could be produced just-in-time directly at the web-presentation by the usage of PHP-scripts, some diagrams require a sophisticated image conversion service.

Diagrams for the CACHEBENCH and the PRIOMARK could be generated by using gnuplot[1]. The repository server produces these diagrams, when receiving a new benchmark result. More exactly, the server extracts the plain ASCII output of the benchmark result to a temporary file and starts a gnuplot-script to convert the benchmark data into a postscript file. In a second step the server converts the postscript file into a ppm-file (portable pixmap file format) using the Netpbm[2]-package. The Netpbm-package enables the conversion into a number of different image formats and provides additional methods in order to manipulate pictures, e.g. rotation. A postscript and a JPEG version of the produced diagram are stored in the MySQL database as LONGBLOB (a binary large object column with a maximum length of 4GB) and could be displayed at the web-presentation.

Error and Exception handling

In case an exception was thrown on the server side, the client will get an XML-message with a detailed failure-output containing a unique failure number, a short failure description and optionally a stack-trace output. The repository server distinguishes between different error code classes (see table 5.2).

Error Code Classes	Description
1.000 – 1.999	Communication-Errors
2.000 – 2.999	Database Errors
3.000 – 3.999	XML Errors
4.000 – 4.999	Logical Errors
5.000 – 7.999	Unused
8.000 – 8.999	Benchmark Client Errors
9.000 – 9.999	Other Errors

Table 5.2: Repository Server: Error Code Classes

Appendix E includes a complete list of all possible error messages.

5.3.3.3 Persistence Layer

Our first persistence architecture concept was based on an object-oriented database, because object-oriented databases appear to be the conceptually most appealing kind of data store with regard to object-oriented programming languages like Java. But as already mentioned, the IPACS web-presentation needs the capability to aggregate different benchmark results in a single table. In order to satisfy this requirement adequately, the usage of a relational database can be recommended. Nevertheless, combining an object-oriented application layer with a relational database leads to the so-called impedance

---

[1]A portable command-line driven interactive data and function plotting utility for Unix, Linux and many other platforms; see www.gnuplot.info/

[2]package of graphics programs and a programming library, see netpbm.sourceforge.net

mismatch that refers to difficulties based on the different conceptual bases (cf. [43] or [44]).

At first glance, the new Java Data Objects (JDO) standard [45] might well be a considerable solution as the persistence layer of choice. JDO is an industry standard for object persistence and intended for the usage with the Java 2 Standard (J2SE) and Enterprise Edition (J2EE). Although JDO provides a standardized and transparent persistence solution including tremendous benefits to application developers, the JDO specification has been discussed controversially in the Java community (see [46]). The criticism concerns, among others, the bytecode enhancement process, the shortcoming of the query language JDOQL, the overlaps between the Enterprise JavaBeans specification and JDO, and, the conceptual design of JDO as a lightweight persistence approach without user authentication or role-based authorization ([47]). These shortcomings and the fact that the few available JDO implementations were not thoroughly tested when the IPACS project started in 2002 are the primary reasons that a JDO approach was finally rejected.

A second approach was based on a proprietary object-relational (O/R) mapping tool. But even if there are well-tested O/R mapping tools like TopLink or Hibernate available, they always lock developers into a particular vendor and lead to restriction in application portability. This leads to the elimination of O/R mapping tools as a persistence approach. But mapping benchmark results and computer information to fixed relational tables with hardcoded SQL/JDBC (Structured Query Language/Java Database Connectivity) leads to a disadvantage regarding flexibility.

Therefore, an individual persistence layer was developed in response to the needs of the IPACS project. Due to ongoing improvements e.g. the further software development of the IPACS benchmarks, the IPACS data model as already presented in figure 5.1 has to be highly adaptable. Changes in the data model e.g. to be responsive to new hardware-architectures may not require any modifications with regard to the Java source code.

Therefore, our persistence approach is based on a XML-mapping file, that has to conserve the integrity of the data model within the database. Moreover, the purpose of the mapping file is to specify all aspects of data transfer, including the structure of the XML message and the structure of the database. In detail, the business layer (cf. section 5.3.3.2) e.g. receives a computer configuration as an IPACS-DTD conform XML message (appendix B). The business layer passes it to a Java class (`configuration`) of the persistence layer that analyzes the XML document with the help of a DOM parser. In order to store the data of the given computer configuration in the database, meta-information like table name and data type has to be looked up for every XML tag in the message describing the computer configuration. With this information, SQL statements are constructed dynamically and all attributes are inserted in the corresponding tables with the help of JDBC-statements. This ensures an easy adaptability of all components to future requirements and furthermore, allows an easy adaption of the database structure e.g. by adding new attributes.

5.4 Web-Presentation and Information Retrieval Component

5.4.1 Organization

The IPACS web server (`www.ipacs-benchmark.org`) provides different views to the benchmark results repository. The decision to publish the benchmark results on a public web server rather than to publish them within the benchmark client environment has been made to keep the software architecture of the client as simple as possible.

The software we chose for the web includes the proven robust combination of the Apache HTTP-Server with PHP scripts to access the MySQL database of the repository. The web pages have been programmed in a highly flexible way. The complete design and the site navigation are defined in one single file, which makes it very comfortable to perform changes affecting the complete site. The same is true for the benchmarks: in order to include a new benchmark into the IPACS environment, the following steps are necessary:

- create the appropriate database tables,

- define the parameters to show in the benchmark specific definition file.

5.4.2 Query Modules

Every benchmark has three levels of detail: a single number, which represents the most condensed result (as the R_{max} of LINPACK), a set of numbers which gives more insight into the performance characteristics (e.g. N_{max}, $N_{1/2}$ in LINPACK) and finally the output of the benchmark run. These three levels are mapped to correspondent web pages.

A page where the user is able to restrict the display of the results by various manual selections, serves as an entry level. Selection parameters include the benchmarks to display and system characteristics like computer architecture, operating system and others (Figure 5.5).

The results are then presented in the most condensed form, together with the main hardware and software characteristics, in an overview table. The visitor can then click on appropriate links to expand more and more details. This approach is also used on other benchmarking activities, e.g. in the web-presentation of the SPEC benchmarks.

A final point in the presentation of the results to consider is the order in which the computer systems are listed. For LINPACK/TOP500 the computers are easily ordered with respect to their R_{max} value. But for IPACS, with more than a dozen different benchmarks, it is not possible to find a meaningful way to order the HPC systems. The IDC tries to define a rank based on a (equal) weighting scheme of the different benchmarks to construct a single number for ordering.

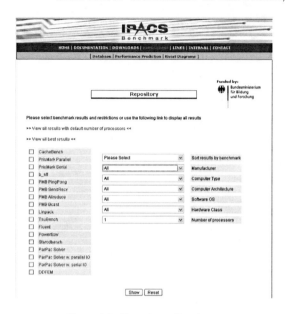

Figure 5.5: Repository Database.

Number of results found with your selection: 30
New selection

(To receive more information abount an entry, please click "View" in the column "Details")

Computer	Details	CacheBench RMW (MB/S)	PrioMark Parallel Disk I/O Performance (MB/s per process)	PMB PingPong Max. Bandwidth (MB/sec)
cheetah IBM IBM pSeries System, Power 4 Center of Computational Sciences 2005-04-26	view	5971.9115	8.854	1524.69
vr-master Linux NetworX PC, cluster Linux NetworX 2005-04-22	view	16762.2397	n/a	849.56
Seaborg IBM SP POWER3, IBM SP Seaborg 2004-06-09	view	2856.1056	n/a	469.27
rumtest6.rz.uni-mannheim.de n/a n/a, x86_64 IT Center University of Mannheim 2006-01-25	view	12298.6363	162.7	432.43
rumtest7.rz.uni-mannheim.de n/a n/a, x68_64 IT Center University of Mannheim 2006-01-25	view	26569.1494	167	426.67
rumtest5.rz.uni-mannheim.de n/a n/a, SMP IT Center Univerity Mannheim 2006-01-30	view	11708.0914	58.2	240.94

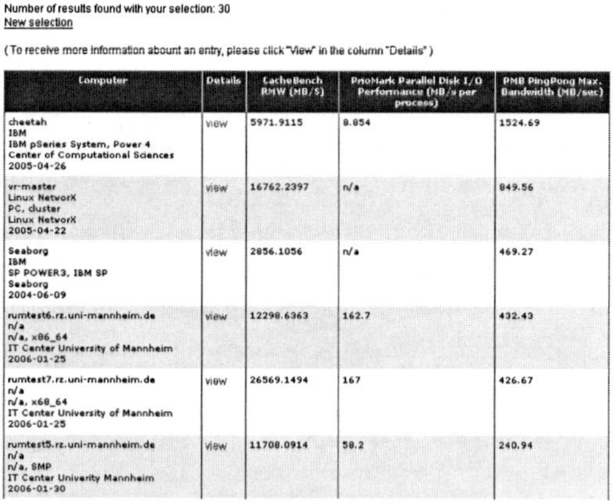

Figure 5.6: Comparison Table.

However, there has been disagreement about this scheme in the scientific benchmark community, as a weight between different performance numbers depends on particular application characteristics. Each visitor has his own applications which imply different importance (or weights) between the numbers of different benchmarks.

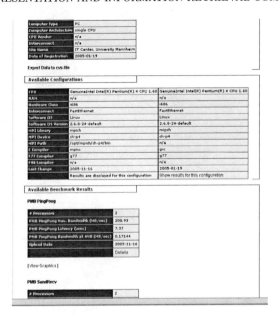

Figure 5.7: Computer and Configuration View.

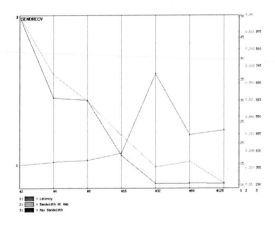

Figure 5.8: SENDRECV for different processor numbers.

Therefore, IPACS will not imply any ordering on the overview of results, but will provide visitors with the option of selecting their own ordering schemes for assessment (e.g. ordering with respect to the results of a specific benchmark, cf. Figure 5.6).

When a user follows a link to a specific system in the overview table, he will be led to the computer and configuration view (Figure 5.7). In this area, besides the hardware

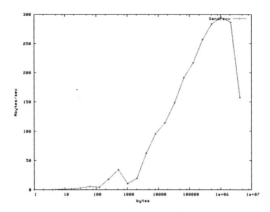

Figure 5.9: SENDRECV, Benchmark Details

characteristics and configuration details, all benchmark results of that system are listed. Additional graphical overviews allow an even more comprehensive view at the different benchmark results (Figure 5.8 and 5.9). There is also the possibility to switch between different stored configurations of the system, if there are any. Finally, visitors can access the original output of a specific benchmark run.

5.4.2.1   Computer Comparison with Kiviat Diagrams

In order to enable the analysis of different benchmark results and several HPCs within the help of one single diagram, we settled on Kiviat charts. A Kiviat chart (also called radar diagram) is best suited to present multivariate data. The outcome of this diagram is a polygon for each computer. Figure 5.12 e.g. represents the measured values of eight benchmark types (ALLREDUCE, BCAST, CACHEBENCH, DDFEM, PINGPONG, SENDRECV, PARPAC Solver and TAUBENCH) and three HPCs (Seaborg, VR-Master and Cheetah). On the basis of its axes, it is possible to compare the computers with regard to the different benchmark results.

Used Techniques

For the creation of the diagrams, PHP was used in connection with the "GD Graphics Library". The whole calculation is done without any external module or library. Subsequently we describe how users compare different computer systems using Kiviat diagrams on the IPACS website.

Web Frontend

Step 1: To perform a computer comparison between different HPCs, one computer has to be selected as source. Therefore, the web frontend generates a list consisting all computers that provide one result for at least three different IPACS benchmarks.

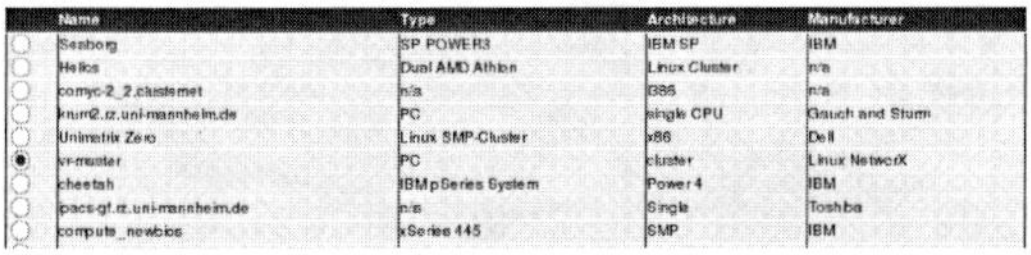

Name	Type	Architecture	Manufacturer
Seaborg	SP POWER3	IBM SP	IBM
Helios	Dual AMD Athlon	Linux Cluster	n/a
comyc-2_2.clustermet	n/a	i386	n/a
krum2.rz.uni-mannheim.de	PC	single CPU	Gnuch and Sturm
Unimatrix Zero	Linux SMP-Cluster	x86	Dell
vr-master	PC	cluster	Linux NetworX
cheetah	IBM pSeries System	Power 4	IBM
ipacs.gf.rz.uni-mannheim.de	n/a	Single	Toshiba
compute_newbios	xSeries 445	SMP	IBM

Figure 5.10: Kiviat Diagram, Step 1.

Step 2: As the second step, all HPCs, which have at least three results of the same IPACS benchmarks as the selected computer are listed. From that list the user can choose any amount of computers (left column in Figure 5.11). Optionally the processor count, for each benchmark, can be specified here (pull down selectors in right columns in Figure 5.11).

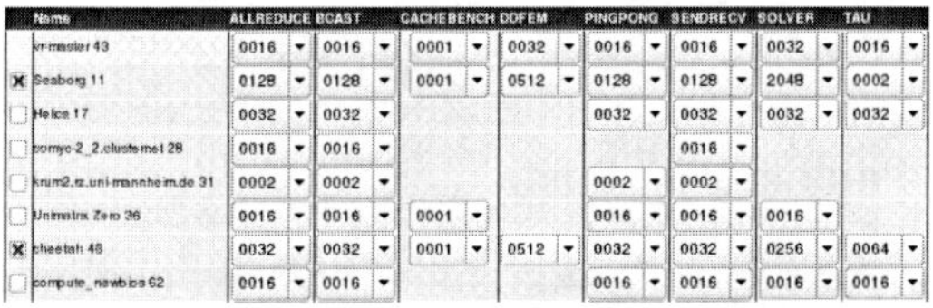

Name	ALLREDUCE	BCAST		CACHEBENCH	DDFEM	PINGPONG	SENDRECV	SOLVER		TAU
vr-master 43	0016	0016	0001		0032	0016	0016	0032		0016
☒ Seaborg 11	0128	0128	0001		0512	0128	0128	2048		0002
Helios 17	0032	0032				0032	0032	0032		0032
comyc-2_2.clustermet 28	0016	0016				0016				
krum2.rz.uni-mannheim.de 31	0002	0002				0002	0002			
Unimatrix Zero 36	0016	0016	0001			0016	0016	0016		
☒ cheetah 46	0032	0032	0001		0512	0032	0032	0256		0064
compute_newbios 62	0016	0016				0016	0016	0016		0016

Figure 5.11: Kiviat Diagram, Step 2.

Step 3: As the last step, all main values will be read from the database. Every ray of the diagram (Figure 5.11) represents a single benchmark and every polygon represents a HPC. The values will be scaled between null and one and after that, they will be plotted on the corresponding ray. In this way, the computer with the highest performance is always at the end of the ray.

5.4.2.2   Performance Prediction

The collection and representation of the data is split into three steps. As the first step, a computer will be chosen from a list. At the second step, the data will be read from the database and can be partly modified here. At the last step the data will be processed and a diagram will be generated. For more information about performance prediction, see also section 3.3.

Step 1: A list of computers will be created. Every computer must come up with the criteria below:

- Available values for a CACHEBENCH benchmark, with one processor

- Available values for a PINGPONG benchmark, with two processors

Once all of the named criteria are fulfilled the HPC can be used for performance prediction.

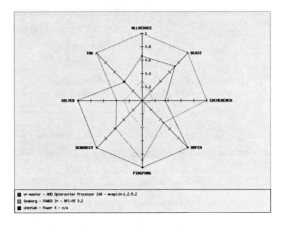

Figure 5.12: Kiviat Diagram of three HPCs.

Name	Type	Architecture	Manufacturer	Insert Date	
Seaborg	SP POWER3	IBM SP	IBM	2004-06-09	View
Unixmatrix Zero	Linux SMP-Cluster	x86	Dell	2005-02-04	View
vr-master	PC	cluster	Linux NetworX	2005-04-22	View
cheetah	IBM pSeries System	Power 4	IBM	2005-04-26	View

Figure 5.13: Performance Prediction, Step 1.

Step 2: At the second step, the corresponding data will be read from the database. Next the script will write the data into different files. Above all, a folder with a unique name will be created. The name of that folder is made up of the current date and the MD5 hash value of the sum of the unix timestamp and a 32 bit random value.

Additionally, it will be checked if the folder does exist. In that, case a new name will be generated till a name was found which doesn't exist yet.

All needed data is listed below:

- CacheBench

    - Read
    - Write
    - Hand Read
    - Hand Write
    - RMW
    - Hand RMW
    - Memset
    - Memcpy

- PINGPONG
    - Max Bandwidth
    - Bandwidth at four MB
    - Latency
- Processor information
    - Name
    - Speed (in GHz)
    - Flops per Cycle

Figure 5.14: Performance Prediction, Step 2.

Step 3: At the last step, the data will be processed from an external program. The output will be written in two external files wherefrom the data will be read from the PHP script. Finally, a diagram will be generated by using the PHP script.

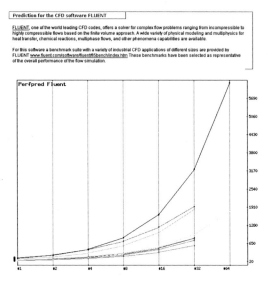

Figure 5.15: Performance Prediction, FLUENT.

5.5   IPACS Client and Execution Framework

As being discussed in the previous chapters the IPACS benchmark environment consists of three central pillars, the IPACS repository, the web interface and the IPACS client. In this section, we present the requirements of the IPACS client. The requirements can be abstracted to a central registration for the HPC to be measured, the download and execution of the IPACS benchmarks and at least the upload of the computed results (Figure 5.16). We will start our presentation of the IPACS client with a short discussion of the different possibilities taken into account in the early analysis phase for a possible architectural design of the client.

5.5.1   Architectural Design Decisions

In the early analysis phase, when we decided which requirements the whole IPACS framework should have, we tried to discover which architectural design models would solve best the requirements of the IPACS client.

5.5.1.1   HTML-Based Client

We had to recognize very early that a web-based client would not be able to fulfill all of the given requirements. A web-based client would easily be able to gather information about a HPC by entering the data in a form, but would not be able to gather the information in an automated way. Also, an execution framework could not be implemented by using an

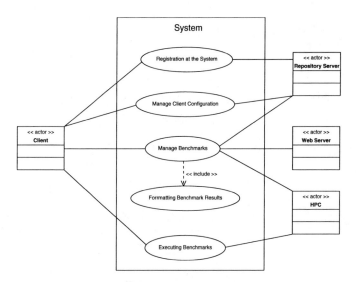

Figure 5.16: Main use case of the IPACS client.

HTML-based solution. Even the usage of *Java Beans* [48] or *JavaScript* [49] in addition to HTML would not solve the problems given.

5.5.1.2 Java Applets

The usage of the technologies *Java Applets* [50], Server Pages [51] and Servlets [41] was taken into account next, but the security restrictions given by Java Applets where e.g. an internet connection to a host, the Applet is not downloaded from, cannot be established due to the security mechanisms of Java, caused that a simple Applet would not be able to fulfill the given requirements of an execution framework, where e.g. the source code of a benchmark should be downloaded and transferred to, installed and executed on a remote HPC.

5.5.1.3 Java WebStart

An easy usage of the client was expected as one of the most important requirements. Therefore, we evaluated different possibilities on how the client could be represented on the IPACS web page. As mentioned above, Java applets have many restriction, not being able to fulfill every one of the expected tasks. Another solution that was taken into account was using Java Web Start [52], but it also has some restrictions e.g. code can only be executed in a sand box on the local system without having access to the systems environment. These restrictions could be circumvented by an agreement of a user to a certificate, allowing access to local environment.

5.5.1.4   Stand-Alone Application

Besides a web based solution, a stand-alone application should be available, too. Therefore, we decided to minimize the redundancy of code by a distinction of the installation
routine, adapted to the technology used and the main application which is equal for all of
them. Executing the installation routine either by using Java Web Start or by downloading a jar file `Client.jar` and executing it in the command line (`java -jar Client.jar`),
the software is installed in the home directory creating a directory named `IPACSclient`
and all needed files are copied to it. In both ways the installation routine ends with an
automated start of the main application.

5.5.2   The IPACS HPC Model and its Representing View

The underlying model describing an HPC and the representation of the model in the
IPACS client is presented in the following section. Having a one-to-one realization of
the model in the GUI, we present the model in association with the representation in its
view.

   As mentioned in the section 5.2 for a later comparison of the executed benchmarks
and their corresponding results, the HPC needs to be registered at the IPACS environment. Therefore, an underlying model was introduced on the client side covering the
most important elements needed for a sufficient description of an HPC. Accordant to
the Model-View-Controller Pattern [53], the model was separated from the representing
view of data. Three main sections were discovered describing an HPC environment: the
site information, the computer information and the computer configuration. In the next
subsections, we shall present an abstract view of the model with its associated view, as
it is currently represented in the IPACS client.

5.5.2.1   Site Information

Two parts are subsumed under the term of the site information: a description of the
location and the person in charge. For the description of the location information like the
name of the situating institute or company, the street, city area or country are needed
(Figure 5.17).

   The person in charge is assumed to be located in the same building, therefore only
information about his or her name, phone number or email address are needed.

5.5.2.2   Client Information

The second part, which needs to be described is the information about mostly non changing parts of the HPC. The values needing to be inserted are the name of the HPC, its
type, its architecture and the manufacturer of the system. Figure 5.18 gives an example
of the corresponding view as it is actually used in the IPACS client.

Figure 5.17: Representing view of the Site Information.

5.5.2.3 Client Configuration

The third and most changing part for an HPC is subsumed under the term of client configuration. The configuration itself is also being separated into two major parts: the hardware and the software settings. An overview is given in the UML class diagram in Figure 5.19.

5.5.2.4 Hardware Settings

The hardware settings consist of three parts: primary hardware settings, CPU settings and memory settings, as it can be seen in the UML class diagram in Figure 5.20.

The primary hardware settings describe the environment of the system. They describe the systems underlying hardware class, how the nodes are connected with each other (inter connect), the number of nodes which are available on the system and the number of processors each node consists of (Figure 5.21).

The CPU settings describe the CPU used on the nodes. The description of a CPU consists of the name of a CPU (e.g AMD Opteron), its vendor (e.g. Intel, AMD) the speed of the CPU, the FLOPS being computed in a cycle and the size of the cache.

The last part in the description of the changeable hardware environment of an HPC is the settings for the available memory, which is being described with the two parameters, RAM type and its size.

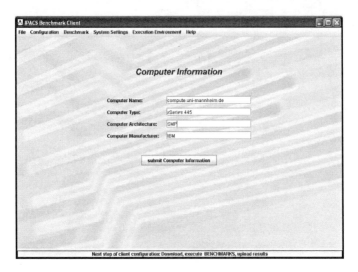

Figure 5.18: Representing view of the Computer Information.

Figure 5.19: UML class diagram of the Computer Configuration.

5.5.2.5   Software Settings

On the description of the software side an HPC consists of, we subsumed it into four major parts: information about the used Message Passing Interface MPI, the available compiler for the specific MPI version, the compiler available on the system and at least information about the underlying operating system. An overview is given in the UML class diagram in Figure 5.22.

The settings available for a description of an MPI are their name, the device used, and the path to the binaries of the described MPI environment.

Each MPI environment has a large number of available compilers, but for the settings only the C and the Cxx compiler are needed.

In addition to the MPI dependant compiler, the IPACS client gives the ability to set standard compiler in the environment, like the old but still used F77 and F90 compilers and a standard C compiler like the gcc.

For the description of the operating system, its name and version are needed.

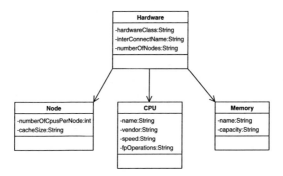

Figure 5.20: UML class diagram of the Hardware class.

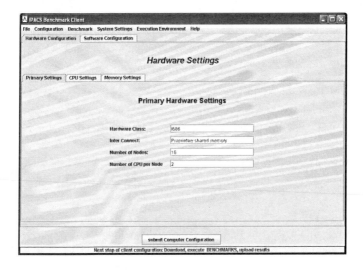

Figure 5.21: View representation of the primary hardware class.

5.5.3 Gathering the HPC's Information

Some of the information needed for registering the HPC at the IPACS environment can be gathered by simply using a script which needs to be executed on the HPC. In this section, we will present the two ways of getting the information needed by using this simple script either directly inside the IPACS client if the client is running on the system under consideration, or manually running the script on a remote system. In both ways, the same script is used. Therefore, we will firstly describe the information the script can get and describe in the following the ways how the scripts are executed as remote or local scripts.

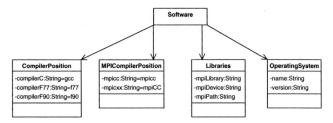

Figure 5.22: UML class diagram of the Software class.

5.5.3.1   System Information Scripts

Even if the underlying operating system of an HPC is actually mostly UNIX-based, in some cases a Windows-based computer could be used as access to the HPC environment. Therefore, we decided to have scripts for both systems, the `sysinfo.sh` for UNIX-based system and a `SystemInformation.bat` for windows-based access nodes, both being discussed in the following.

UNIX-Based Access Nodes

The script uses shell commands available on UNIX systems (without any restrictions) to get information about the hostname, the user, the memory of the system, and information about available CPUs (listing 5.6). The gathered information is written to a text file named `info.txt`. This file is then used by the client in order to add the information to the HPC model, making them visible in its GUI representation.

```
echo "SystemInformation Linux" >infos.txt
echo "ausgabe von hostname"      >>infos.txt
hostname -f                      >>infos.txt
echo "ausgabe von uname"         >>infos.txt
uname -a                         >>infos.txt
echo "ausgabe von df"            >>infos.txt
df -h                            >>infos.txt
echo "ausgabe von meminfo"       >>infos.txt
cat /proc/meminfo                >>infos.txt
echo "ausgabe von cpuinfo"       >>infos.txt
cat /proc/cpuinfo                >>infos.txt
echo "ausgabe von version"       >>infos.txt
cat /proc/version                >>infos.txt
```

Listing 5.6: sysinfo.sh

Windows-Based Access Nodes

A similar script as the previous described script for UNIX based systems is used for Windows access nodes. The following code block (Listing 5.7) shows the commands executed on the Windows system: first information about the hostname, the current user, information of the available memory and at least information of the CPU are gathered and piped to the sysinfosWin.txt which is then parsed by the client to add the information to the HPC description model.

```
echo SystemInformation Windows >sysinfosWin.txt


echo Ausgabe von Hostname      >>sysinfosWin.txt
hostname                       >>sysinfosWin.txt


echo Ausgabe von meminfo       >>sysinfosWin.txt
mem                            >>sysinfosWin.txt


echo Ausgabe von cpuinfo(reg)  >>sysinfosWin.txt
reg Query HKEY_LOCAL_MACHINE\Hardware\Description\
    System\CentralProcessor\0 /v
    ProcessorNameString        >>sysinfosWin.txt


echo Ausgabe von systeminfo    >>sysinfosWin.txt
systeminfo                     >>sysinfosWin.txt


echo finished getting systemInformation
```

Listing 5.7: SystemInformation.bat

5.5.3.2 Gathering System Information Using the IPACS Client

Using the IPACS client, two possibilities arise when information about the system under consideration is gathered and inserted into the IPACS client. As mentioned above, the script can be executed directly using the IPACS client but also as a stand-alone script. In both ways, text files with the information about the systems are generated as it is described in the previous sections. These text files are then parsed by the IPACS client and the information is transformed according to the underlying HPC model presented in section 5.5.2.

In a first step, the user can easily start the script using the IPACS client. The client then starts a new job on the actual system, executing one of the previously described scripts according to the underlying operating system (Figure 5.23).

If a user decided to get information from a remote system, he needs to copy the script to the system under consideration corresponding to the underlying operating system, executing the script and then copying the information text file back to the system the client is being executed on. In this situation the user is able to execute the insertion of the data to the IPACS HPC data model by pressing the "load System Information" menu item (Figure 5.23). The information text file is then parsed and the received data is added

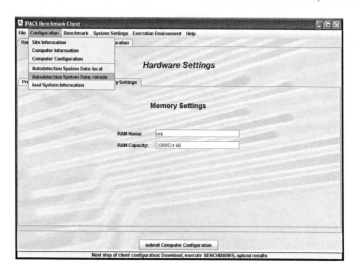

Figure 5.23: Auto detection of the underlying system environment.

to the HPC model. Using the local auto detection, the last step is directly executed by the client.

5.5.4   Data Storage

After having submitted the data for the three sections site information, computer information and computer configuration, this information is stored in the repository for a later comparison of measured systems. On the local system, only a universal ID assigned by the repository is stored avoiding redundant data storage. This unique ID enables the IPACS client to request his latest submitted configuration from the repository server at each starting procedure. For the communication with the repository server, an XML-based communication process is used being described in the section 5.3.3.1.

5.5.5   Benchmarks

Having inserted all needed information describing an HPC environment, the user is able to download and execute the benchmarks available in the IPACS benchmark suite. In this section, we present either the download but also the transformation of the results of the executed benchmarks according to the data model used on the repository server and its view, how the results are represented on the IPACS web-presentation after being uploaded. In a later section, we describe the execution environment (5.5.6) which provides an easy installation, execution and gathering of the benchmark results.

5.5.5.1 Benchmark Download

Using the IPACS client, a user can easily select one of the available benchmarks of the IPACS environment. The client provides a short description of the selected benchmark appearing in the standard web browser of the system and a button for an easy download of the source code for a selected benchmark (Figure 5.24).

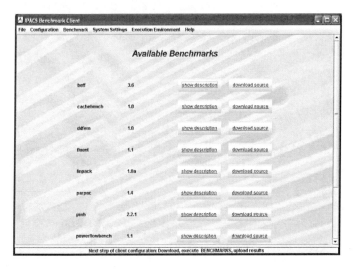

Figure 5.24: Available Benchmarks.

5.5.5.2 Executing Benchmarks by Hand

How the benchmarks of the IPACS environment are executed by hand is described in section 5.6 and is also available in the client's help section, describing the steps required for each of the available benchmarks, which are documented for the Helics cluster ([54]), but also valid for most of the systems.

After the execution of the benchmarks, their results need to be copied to the system the client is running on for the purpose of an advanced processing.

5.5.5.3 Benchmark Results and Result Converter

In the result set of every IPACSbenchmark, one principal value can be identified. Besides this principal value, additional, at most five second-level values can be identified characterizing the HPC for this specific benchmark. Therefore, the conversion of the benchmark results is one of the central parts of the IPACS client.

In the benchmark section, the user can easily select a result file which should be uploaded to the IPACS repository server. As a first step, the result file is read and the information available is inserted into a `StringBuffer` object, being passed to the

ResultManager, which tries to map the result file to a benchmark. Having successfully mapped the results to one of the benchmarks, the result buffer is passed to the specific benchmark result converter. The task of the result converter is to identify the corresponding values for the executed benchmark. Each of the available benchmark result converter is derived from an abstract converter, providing only one implementation of the recurring code. For the purpose of identifying and extracting the values in the result file, regular expressions are used. Figure 5.25 gives a representation of the ResultManager and the associated Converter interface with all actually available realizations of this interfaces represented as an UML class diagram.

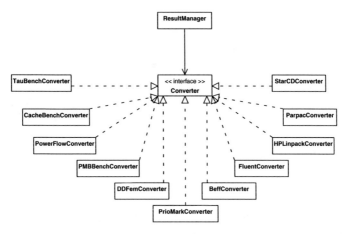

Figure 5.25: UML class diagram of the ResultManager class.

After the identification of the representing values in a benchmark result file a conversion corresponding to the result DTD (DTD can be found in appendix B) is made. The resulting XML-based document is then ready for transmission to the repository server, which is done in the next step.

5.5.5.4   Comparison of the Benchmark Results

After the transmission of the results for a specific benchmark to the repository server, the own result is displayed in comparison with other benchmark results regarding to the principal value of the benchmark. The comparison is displayed as an HTML page provided by the web server, displaying it in the standard browser of the local system (5.4)

5.5.6   Execution Framework

Besides the possibility of manually downloading and executing the benchmarks of the IPACS benchmark suite, for some of the benchmarks an automated script is available configuring and executing the benchmark according to the HPC. How the configuration and execution process is implemented, is being described in the section 6.2. In this section, we shall present the GUI representation of the execution framework used in the IPACS client suite.

5.5.6.1 Execution Framework Settings

For the automated installation and execution of the benchmarks, additional setting information is needed. Therefore, the user first needs to select one of the automated benchmarks to be executed as it can be seen in Figure 5.26. Currently, five benchmarks TAUBENCH, PMB, DDFEM, B_{eff} and PARPACBENCH are available for this purpose. The other available benchmarks of the IPACS benchmark suite will be also added in near future.

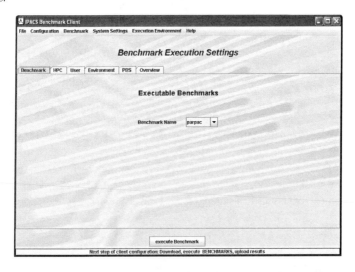

Figure 5.26: Executable benchmarks in the execution framework.

In the next tabs, information like the address of the HPC host node, the username of the executing user on this system are required for getting the ability to connect with the system.

The paths where the source code of the benchmark should be downloaded to on the local system, the location where the benchmark should be installed on the HPC system and where the benchmark results should be copied to after execution need to be specified in the tab "Environment" (Figure 5.27).

At least the settings of the batch system used on the HPC need to be specified if some is available, else the user needs to specify that the benchmark should be executed directly. If a batch system is used, the commands for submitting a job (e.g. qsub for *PBS*) and the command for getting current information about the job (e.g. qstat for *PBS*) need to be added. Besides the name of the queue, the job should be added to, additional and

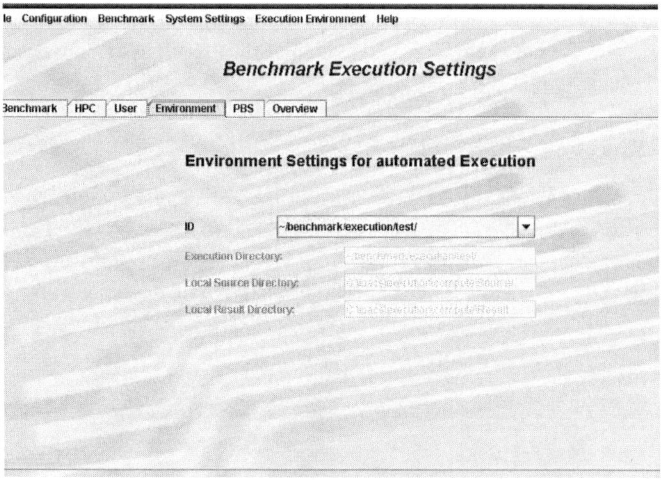

Figure 5.27: HPC environment description in the execution framework.

specific information of the system can be specified (e.g. the walltime used for the queue) and are inserted in the generated job script during the configuration and make process as it is described in section 6.2.

In the last tab available, an overview of the current settings is given. If the user stores the settings on the local system, at the next starting of the IPACS client the stored settings are read and added to the model used for displaying it in the presented GUI view.

5.5.6.2 Preparing the Execution on the HPC

Having added the needed information, the user can execute the benchmark on the specified HPC. For this purpose, an ssh connection to the system is established by using the jsch-API [55]. The directories specified in the environment settings are created on the local and on the remote system in the next step. If the source code in the most actual version of the selected benchmark is not available on the local source directory, it is downloaded from the IPACS repository and copied to the source directory specified for the HPC. How the benchmark is automatically configured according to the underlying HPC environment is described in the section (cf. section 6.2) as well as the next steps for making and running the benchmark. Figure 5.28 gives an example of the output on the HPC either of the standard output stream (black) or the error stream (red). If the installation and execution process are started successfully on the HPC the user gets displayed the job ID for the current execution. If benchmarks are executed for a different number of nodes, each will be executed in a single job (Figure 5.28).

Figure 5.28: HPC Output for the make command of the PARPAC\textsc{Bench}.

5.5.6.3   Gathering the Benchmark Results

The execution of a benchmark takes a few minutes depending on the benchmark, number of nodes and the environment of the HPC. After the start of the execution of a specific benchmark, the job IDs are added to a table listing all the executed jobs where the user did not try to download the benchmark results. If a benchmark is executed with multiple numbers of nodes, the execution is treated as a single transaction because the results are written in the same result file and a redundant collection of the same result should therefore be avoided (Figure 5.29). If the user decides to download the results on the remote system, it is checked if, in case of a single job it is finished or, in case of a transaction consisting of multiple jobs, all of them are finished. If the results are available, these are packed to a tar file and copied to the local result path as it is specified in the environment settings. After successfully downloading the results to the local system, the files are unpacked and the result files are read and passed to the result converter as it was described in the section 5.5.5.3. The automated upload of the results to the repository server and the display of the results in comparison to the available benchmark results are the last steps in the execution and gathering process.

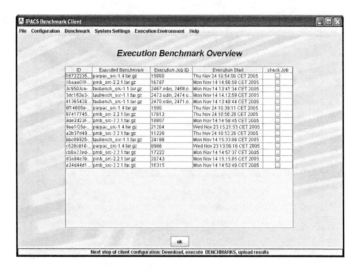

Figure 5.29: Recently executed benchmarks with the execution environment.

5.6   System Evaluation from a users perspective

In this section, we will evaluate the IPACS architecture by executing several benchmarks of the IPACS benchmark suite (cf. section 3.2) in a test environment. The system evaluation is primarily focused on the IPACS client (cf. section 5.5) and the IPACS benchmarks. The test environment consists of two different HPCs: the Helics Cluster and the Compute System.

On the one hand, the Helics Cluster at the IWR of the University of Heidelberg (`http://helics.iwr.uni-heidelberg.de/`) consists of 512 AMD Athlon MP processors with 256 nodes. A Debian GNU/Linux is installed and a low level GM driver is needed for the Myricom hardware. Torque, an OpenPBS derivative is used as the batch system. The Moab scheduler on top of torque optimizes the utilization of HELICS. Mpich is used for parallel programming. On the other hand, the Compute System at the University of Mannheim is a SuSE-Linux installation with 16 Intel XEON Hyperthreading processors. Mpich is installed and it operates without a batch system.

The IPACS client handles both HPCs; the system settings can be mostly auto-detected, but some values have to be completed by the user. The download of benchmarks and the upload of benchmark results work without any exceptions. Evaluations are then shown within the IPACS-Repository in a web-browser. For some benchmarks, special configurations are needed, because not all support automated installation. Also, different external programs, like PETSc for the DDFEM-benchmark, must be installed manually. But most of the benchmarks can be installed, compiled and started self-controlled with the execution framework (cf. section 5.5.6). The results are then stored automatically in the IPACS repository (cf. section 5.3).

The main difference concerning the practical use between the two test-environments is the scheduling of jobs. The Helics Cluster queues jobs with PBS. Jobs for the Compute System are started directly "by hand". Also, the various compilers on both systems have to be discriminated. With the IPACS client, you can choose which compiler you want to use by editing the compiler value in the software settings section.

5.6.1 IPACS Environment

In this section, we will give an introduction in the usage of the IPACS client. First, the client has to be downloaded at `www.ipacs-benchmark.org`. Then it is started with `java -jar Client.jar` (with Java WebStart, these steps can be automated). This will create the IPACS client directory, in which personal settings are saved. Also, the client automatically pops up.

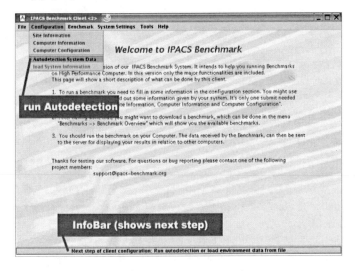

Figure 5.30: On the bottom of the IPACS client there is a status bar. It shows the next steps in how to work with the client.

A welcome screen (Figure 5.30) with a short entering guide will appear. If the client is connected via a proxy with the internet, this can be set up and tested here. Also remote access to the HPC is specified now. After finishing the introduction, the HPC system configurations and contact information are set up in the IPACS client. Now, the autodetection will run to let the IPACS client detect most of the HPC system properties. Then, the contact information has to be filled in the corresponding form (Figure 5.31). It is used to distinguish between different benchmarkers on the same site.

Now, the contact person information and computer information have to be entered the same way (like illustrated in Figure 5.32). These entries are not necessarily needed

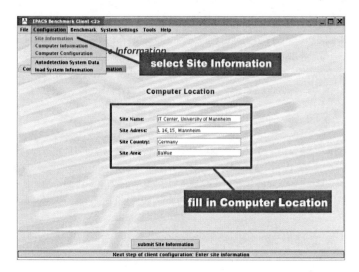

Figure 5.31: Site Name: Name of the Institute/Organization the HPC is related to, Site Address: Address of the Institute/Orgranisation, Site Country: Country of the Institute/Orgranisation, Site Area: State/Region/Area in this Country.

to start the benchmarks but should be entered to let other users know which system is benchmarked and who to contact for further questions or suggestions.

In case the autodetection wasn't able to recognize all computer configuration entries, missing information must be added by typing. The Hardware Configuration will be mostly autodetected. The compiler which the execution framework uses is specified with the mpicc/mpicxx Compiler entry at MPI Compiler Settings and the MPI Path value from the MPI Settings, both parts of the Software Configuration.

Having set up the IPACS client, it is now possible to download, execute and upload the different benchmarks. The execution framework will automate these steps, which will be explained below.

5.6.1.1   Manual Benchmarking

Benchmarks can be selected using the client menu. A click on "Available Benchmarks" shows the several test-programs in a list each with a short description (Figure 5.34). Now the chosen benchmark can be downloaded directly to the HPC.

The next step after downloading the benchmarks is compiling and running them, which will be explained individually for each one in the next chapter. In general, an MPI-implementation has to be chosen which is mostly specified with the full path to the mpicc/mpicxx-compiler-file. This is set up in a configuration file for the benchmark. Then, the Make-script creates the executable file. Now, the appropriate mpirun-command

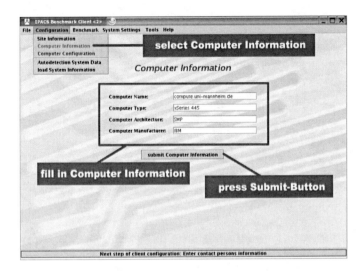

Figure 5.32: Computer Name: The (Network-Node) Name of the HPC, Computer Type: e.g. XSeries 445, Computer Architecture: e.g. SMp or Cluster, Computer Manufacturer: e.g. IBM.

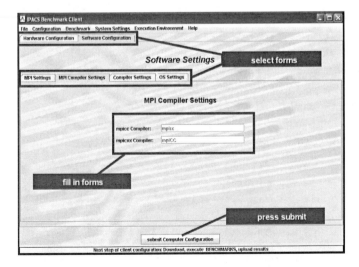

Figure 5.33: The Software Settings are also used for the Execution Framework.

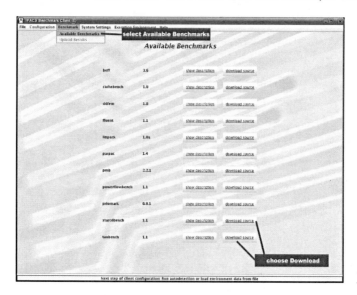

Figure 5.34: Having set up the IPACS client, it is now possible to download the benchmark files.

runs the benchmark. If a batch system is used on the HPC, a script file with the mpiexec-job must be queued. It can be proceeded with one benchmark in a time, i.e. prepare of CACHEBENCH, run and analyze of CACHEBENCH then continue with PRIOMARK.

In order to upload the results, the Upload Results entry in the Benchmarks menu is chosen. In the new window the several result-files are selected (Figure 5.35). Once the upload has finished (and all computations on the IPACS server have been performed), the client will open a browser window which shows the submitted results in comparison to others.

5.6.1.2 Automated Benchmarking

The execution framework simplifies the whole benchmark process. Download and upload proceed fully automatically, compiling and running is administrated via menus. The framework handles the remote access to the HPC. The user name and SSH connection can be entered. If needed, a batch system is specified. All entries can be displayed in an overview. It is possible to test and save all settings. Switching between the different benchmarks comes off with one click. Also all started or running benchmarks are listed in a summary.

Selecting the Execute Benchmark entry in the execution framework launches the automated process (Figure 5.36). Here, a benchmark can be chosen. Already entered configurations is kept for every other benchmark. Switched on the HPC and User flag, the

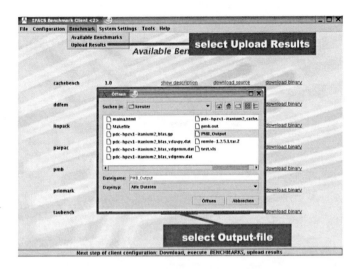

Figure 5.35: By clicking on the "Upload Result" button, uploading the benchmark results is now easily possible.

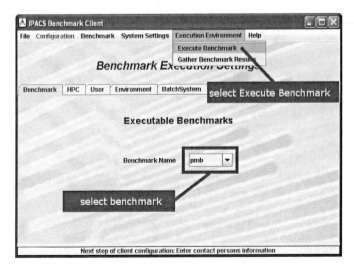

Figure 5.36: Selecting a Benchmark by using the Benchmark Execution Framework.

connection to the benchmarked system is set up. In the batch system entry the queuing can be managed if needed. Every single frame saves the information of its block after the *add*-button was pressed. The last frame shows the overview of the whole selection which was made (Figure 5.37).

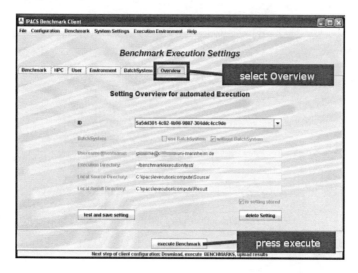

Figure 5.37: Starting the Build- and Execution Process of a Benchmark by using the Benchmark Execution Framework.

Now, the *test* and *save* buttons create a universal ID for the run. It also determines the result in the "Gather Benchmark Results" window. After pushing the "Execute Benchmark" button only the password for the SSH-Connection and the number of processors which will be tested have to be entered. Now a window will pop up with the output of the HPC. The executed commands are shown and the user can observe the compilation and start of the benchmark. After a benchmark is successfully compiled, the Job-ID appears in the output-window (Figure 5.38). It is possible to consecutively proceed with different benchmarks.

Finally, the started and running benchmarks are listed in the Gather Benchmarks Results list (Figure 5.39). Starting time and IDs are displayed; and by checking several benchmarks the status of the process is shown or the output is uploaded automatically. Then, the results concerning the remaining results of the IPACS repository will pop up in a browser window.

5.6.2   Benchmark Tests

The IPACS project provides a comprehensive benchmark suited. Each benchmark requires different installation steps which will be illustrated in detail in the following para-

Figure 5.38: Build- and Execution Process of a Benchmark by using the Benchmark Execution Framework.

graphs. Some parts however are universally valid such as compiler-setting and starting a job. Those will be explained below.

5.6.2.1 Manual Execution

The main focus in setting up one of the different IPACS benchmarks is finding the correct adjustments for the mpi-compiler. In general the make-command creates most of the settings. Many benchmarks will find the mpi-compiler automatically with `./configure`. If not, a config-file which includes variables for the mpi-environment must be edited (i.e. `MPICC=/opt/mpich/ch-p4/bin/mpicxx`). Sometimes the makefile contains this variable or it can be transmitted as parameter with the configure-command. If compilation runs without an error the created executable can then be started corresponding to the HPC-environment.

On the one hand, if no batch system is used, the mpirun command starts the benchmark-executable. With the `-np` parameter the number of processors is specified (i.e. `/opt/mpich/ch-p4/bin/mpirun -np 16 ./anybench`). In the case of different

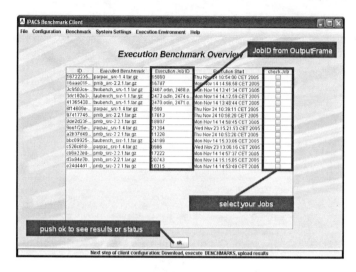

Figure 5.39: Gather Benchmark Results list shows status of started Benchmarks.

mpich-implementations, it is necessary to start the benchmark with the mpirun-command of the same implementation to which it was compiled. On the other hand, if jobs are queued in a batch system a script has to be created that contains the environment settings for the run and the mpiexec-command which will start the benchmark. PBS arguments can be put into the script with #PBS comments. For example #PBS -q odin defines the queue and/or server to which the job will be submitted. #PBS -l defines the resources that are required by the job. The benchmark program can be started in the script with mpiexec which works most likely the same as mpirun. The used communicator / compiler can be specified with the -comm mpich-gm attribute.

```
#!/bin/bash
#PBS -q @odin                          <--- defines the queue
#PBS -l nodes=16:ppn=2:helics,
       walltime=00:30:00.00            <--- defines the resources
##################
cd ~/benchmarks/TauBench/...
echo "job started"
mpiexec -comm mpich-p4 -np 32
       ./TauBench -n 250000 -s 10 <--- runs the job
echo "job finished"
##################
```

Listing 5.8: Example of a PBS-run-script

The script is then submitted with the `qsub` command. `Qstat` or `xpbs` allow to check the status of the job in the queue. Some cluster environments do not support the make-command. In this case, needed commands from the `run`-part of the makefile are put into the script.

Now, we will discuss the manual execution of different IPACS benchmarks in detail. CACHEBENCH is easy to configure because it runs with only one processor. The make command sets up the computer architecture, i.e. `make linux`. Afterwards only the C++-compiler has to be adjusted in the sys.def-file. The `ResultPrefix` value in `user.def` should be changed for a correct naming of the output-file. Then, the benchmark can be compiled and started with make (`make compile`, `make run`). The output is written to the `results/` directory.

The PRIOMARK benchmark is easy to compile. Either the path to the mpi-compiler home directory is edited in the makefile or it is passed as parameter for the make-command (`MPI_HOME = /opt/mpich/ch-p4`). Then, make should create the `priomark`-executable which can be started with mpirun or mpiexec. The output has to be redirected with `>` to any result file (i.e. `mpiexec -np 16 priomark > prio_16cpu.out`).

After unpacking the PMB benchmark the `./configure`-command in the source directory (`src/`) should set up a correct makefile. Then, make creates the `PMB_MPI1` executable. Now, just the run-script in the RUN directory has to be executed. If the mpirun-command cannot be found, the appropriate `mpich-bin`-directory must be added to the PATH-environment-variable (i.e. `export PATH=$PATH:/opt/mpich/ch-p4/bin`). The result is written into `/RUN/PMB_Output`.

TAUBENCH can be fully compiled automatically by using the `./configure`-command and afterwards the `make`-command. If some settings could not be found, the makefile has to be edited in order to set the correct path to compilers (e.g. for ethernet mpich: `CC=/opt/mpich/ch-p4/bin/mpicc`, `LD=/opt/mpich/ch-p4/bin/mpicc`, `INCLUDE=-I ./-I/opt/mpich/ch-p4/include`, `LIBS=-L/opt/mpich/ch-p4/lib -lm`). Now, the executable can be run with the mpirun or mpiexec command. Output has to be redirected with `>` to an output-file (i.e. `mpiexec -np 16 taubench -n 100000 -s 10 > taubench_16cpus.out`).

For the LINPACK benchmark, an efficient BLAS-library is needed. If none is installed, ATLAS can be downloaded (`http://math-atlas.sourceforge.net`). First, a setup file from the `setup/`-directory according to the used system must be copied into the main directory (i.e. `cp setup/Make.Linux_PII_CBLAS Make.Compute_CBLAS`). Then, the path to the BLAS-library (LAdir, LAinc and LAlib variables) and the mpi-compiler (MPdir) must be edited in the standard setup file. The `ARCH` variable must specify the setup file, i.e. `ARCH=Compute_CBLAS` for a setup file with the name `Make.Compute_CBLAS`. Also the TOPdir variable has to be adjusted to the directory where linpack was unzipped. Now the make-command with the appropriate arch parameter starts compiling (i.e. `make arch=Compute_CBLAS`). Afterwards, the executable is in the bin subdirectory specified with its arch name. The benchmark can now be completed as it is done usually, namely by redirecting the output to a result file.

After unpacking the PARPAC benchmark, only the correct path to the mpi-compilers in the `config.ipacs` file has to be set. Then make creates the executable PARPACBENCH which is executed as usually. The output is saved in the result directory.

The DDFEM benchmark, can only be executed with PETSc 2.1.6 which can be downloaded at `http://www-unix.mcs.anl.gov/petsc/`. First, the `PETSC_DIR` environment variable with the correct PETSc installation path must be exported. Then, make should create the executable `./fe` which can now be started with the appropriate arguments, normally `-i 33 -j 33 -k 33 -x 3 -y 3 -z 3 -b 4`. The output should be redirected to a result file.

5.6.2.2   Automated Execution

For the benchmark, which can be executed automatically, it is only necessary to fill the correct mpi-compiler in the IPACS-Client settings (cf. section 5.6.1). Then the Execution Framework has to be configured according to the benchmarked HPC (cf. section 5.6.1.2). Having accomplished these steps once, pressing the execute button will bring the result for the selected benchmark.

5.6.3   Evaluation Summary

Concluding, the IPACS environment makes the measurement of an HPC with the several benchmarks considerably easier. The overhead in downloading the client, completing the forms and running the execution-framework is worthwhile, regarding the costs for manually installing, compiling, and executing all the benchmarks.

The advantage in using the IPACS client is, besides the comfortable measurement of data, the automatic cataloging of the HPC environment, which produced the different results. Also, the direct comparison of the results with the whole IPACS-Repository when the results are uploaded makes a conclusion easier. The user has to insert the system information only once at the beginning. Also, the whole compilation and execution settings are edited once and then used for all benchmarks. So, many recurring steps and difficulties can be avoided.

Chapter 6

T-Systems Solutions for Research GmbH

6.1 TauBench

TAUBENCH is a parallel pseudo benchmark. The original TAU FLOW SOLVER is a three dimensional parallel hybrid multigrid solver, which uses a finite volume scheme in order to solve the Reynolds-averaged Navier-Stokes equations. It is working with hybrid, unstructured or structured grids.

6.1.1 Motivation

The benchmark itself is meant to mimic the run-time performance of the TAU solver. The structure of TAU and TAUBENCH will be outlined more in detail in the following subsections.

The TAU FLOW SOLVER

The code is composed of these independent modules: a preprocessing module, the solver and a grid adaptation module. The preprocessing module is decoupled from the solver. Preprocessing steps like grid partitioning and calculation of the metrics can thus be done on a dedicated preprocessor platform. The decoupled solver therefore can handle large scale calculations on distributed memory machines with limited local memory. The third module is used for grid adaptation. It detects regions with insufficient grid resolution and performs local grid refinement. The initial solution is interpolated to the adapted grid. The flow variables of TAU are stored in the vertices's of the initial grid. Temporal gradients are discretized using a multi-step Runge-Kutta scheme. In order to accelerate the convergence and to steady state, a local time-stepping concept is employed. The gradients of the flow variables are determined by employing a Green-Gauß formula. Alternatively, a central method with either scalar or matrix dissipation can be employed. The viscous fluxes are discretized using central differences. Several turbulence models have been incorporated for this solver. The flow solver TAU has become one of the standard tools in the European aerospace industry and is still actively developed. For a more detailed description we refer to e.g. [56].

6.1.2   Implementation

The scalable Benchmark TauBench is a pseudo benchmark. It emulates the runtime behavior of the Tau Flow Solver with respect to memory footprint and floating point performance. In order to accomplish this, a run time profile of the Tau Flow Solver has been generated. After analyzing the profile, the actual loop structure of the most CPU consuming kernels has been duplicated. TauBench therefore can predict the performance of the Tau Flow Solver not only with respect to machine properties like memory bandwidth or cache latencies, but also with respect to the quality of compilers. As a typical example, we can mention the problem of unrolling/resolving short inner loops and invariant ifs. In order to help the compiler with this task, directives can be inserted by changing the corresponding header files.

Since Tau is an unstructured grid solver, its most important property with respect to performance is the fact that all accesses to the grid are indirect. On the one hand, this in general causes performance degradation, since e.g. prefetches cannot be applied easily. On the other hand, this fact has been exploited by the developers in the implementation. The preprocessor can optimize the grid for cache architectures. The MPI domains themselves are divided into – minimally connected – subgrids. The size of these subgrids is chosen so that the corresponding data fits into one of the caches of the cache-hierarchy – typically the 2nd level is chosen here. Strip mining then is applied. Since the blocks are minimally connected, the grid points can be renumbered and the data thus at the same time is also blocked with respect to cachelines and the associated caches. In addition to that, the preprocessor can generate a grid, which is suitable for vector machines. The preprocessor then generates subgrids in which the memory accesses within the subgrids are mutually exclusive.

In contrast, the pseudo benchmark TauBench does not use a preprocessor. Instead, the code generates an artificial grid. The features of cache-blocking and strip-mining thus also had to be included into the code. To this end, the typical memory access pattern of an optimized grid has been analyzed and implemented. The feature of vector-colored grids can be used by changing the compile directives in the corresponding header files. Last but not least, the MPI communication had to be re-implemented. Since the communication in the original solver uses non-blocking sends/receives for boundary exchanges – overlapped with an occasional MPI-allreduce – the implementation is straightforward. In order to obtain a scalable benchmark, the grid size per processor remains constant. The total grid size thus scales with the number of processors used.

6.1.3   Results

As a test for the accuracy of prediction for TAUBENCH, a wide spectrum of platforms and compilers has been examined. Given the complexity of the problem the comparison of the runtime shows an excellent agreement (see Figure 6.1).

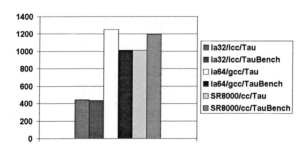

Figure 6.1: TAUBENCH

Most modern computational fluid dynamics (CFD) solvers rely on unstructured grids. This implies that all accesses to main memory are indirect. Since this is the main bottleneck for this type of application, TAUBENCH is well suited as a generic unstructured grid CFD Benchmark within the IPACS framework.

6.2   Benchmark Execution Framework

6.2.1   Motivation

As has been shown in the description of the client, the benchmark execution framework can be separated in two major parts: the benchmark client, which acts as a mediator between the user and the benchmark repository, and the execution part, which handles the installation and execution of the available benchmarks.

In the IPACS execution framework, an execution part was needed, which would be able to compile, build and run the benchmarks in a fully automatic mode on all target platforms. In order to do this, such an execution system needs to analyze, understand, and use the local system infrastructure. The analysis has to cover compilers, the system header files and libraries, the local filesystems, the MPI implementation and, last but not least, the batch system.

Independent from the IPACS project, such an execution framework can be of great value to the HPC community and especially to the Grid community. The reason is that in most Grid software stacks, the burden of porting and deploying applications still remains on the side of the user. Despite the fact that the workflow of the applications is independent from the underlying production platform, the corresponding batch scripts still need to be adapted manually.

In contrast to this, in a Grid environment applications are supposed to run in a fully automatic mode on all grid resources a broker provides. To this day, there is thus a big gap between the grid middleware and the applications themselves.

The IPACS execution framework is able to bridge that gap.

6.2.2   Implementation

The basic functionality of all batch systems has common denominators. Also, the workflow of the applications is – typically – independent from the underlying platforms. If we can find an abstraction of both the workflow (via batch script) and the HPC environment (via configure), this will open the way towards a generic compile and execution environment, which can run on all platforms.

The execution framework has been implemented as a straightforward extension of the gnu autotools. However, instead of the classical `./configure; make; make install` we aim for `./configure; make; make run`   ⋮

The configure step needs to detect and analyze the mpi environment, the filesystems and the batch system. In passing, we note that some of these subsystems are not trivial to analyze – the software thus needs to provide a way to override and supplement the configure findings with corresponding environment variables – MPICC would be an easy example. A non-trivial example would be the detection of parallel queues, which are available for the users.

We note that, sometimes, such a detection might be impossible: However – since we provide a way of how to supplement the information configure detects, the abstraction of the HPC environment (an environment variable QUEUE in the latter case) is a big step ahead.

Once the information is complete, the configure step translates the generic workflow of the application into a specific batch script. `make run` then submits this script into a proper queue.

6.2.2.1   The GNU autotools

The GNU autotools (`autoconf`, `automake` and `libtool`) are the de-facto standard for portably building Fortran, C and C++ applications. They support all UNIX platforms as well as Microsoft Win32. As far as the installer is concerned, building the program depends on nothing but a Bourne shell implementation, a C compiler and a standard "make" program.

`autoconf`[1] performs some system-wide tests to check for common system parameters: the location of programs, the existence of functions and system calls, their behavior, the

---

[1] http://www.gnu.org/software/autoconf

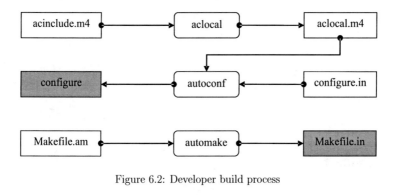

Figure 6.2: Developer build process

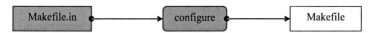

Figure 6.3: User build process

availability of libraries, etc. Using this, it builds (on each target system) an appropriate makefile and a header file, which can be used to build the package natively.

A typical build process on the developer side (using the GNU autotools) includes the steps shown in Figure 6.2. The typical build process on the user side then takes the structure presented in Figure 6.3.

6.2.2.2 The Extension of the Functionality of GNU autotools

In order to provide the functionality we needed for the IPACS execution framework, extending the GNU autotools with respect to e.g. batch systems and MPI was necessary. The implementation is done in standard fashion via a general purpose tool for processing text: M4.

The M4 macros themselves, on the other hand, rely on a modular mechanism: For every batch system and for every MPI version, there is an autonomous shell script, which – when called – is able to detect wether its version matches the installed batch system / MPI version. These scripts also know how to handle the details of the subsystems, e.g.: how to write batch script headers or how to build the proper MPI machinefiles with the information obtained from the batch system during run-time.

Figure 6.4 shows the typical build process for the IPACS execution framework.

6.2.2.3 Build-Time Adaption of the Batch Script

In this build process, the following variables in the above source files (.in) are adapted:

@MPI_VERSION@ Implementation, device and version of MPI. Has to match one of the supported MPI versions.

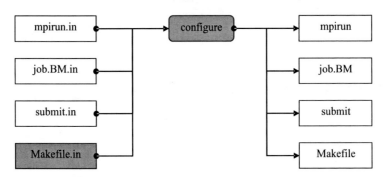

Figure 6.4: IPACS execution framework build process

@MPI_BIN_PATH@ Path to the bin directory of the MPI version.

@NODE_NUM_PROCS@ Number of procs per node.

@BATCH_SYSTEM@ Implementation of the batch system (PBS/Grid Engine etc.). Has to match one of the supported batch systems.

@PROC_ARRAY@ Specific to IPACS. An array of processor numbers for which the benchmark is run.

@QSUB@ Command for submission of the job into a queue.

@QCONF@ Command for status information of queues.

@QUEUE@ The target queue for the application.

@BL1-6@ The batch script header. 6 Lines are supported.

@SCRDIR@ Local scratch directory. Needed for I/O critical applications.

@CONFIGDIR@ The directory in which the build process takes place.

In addition to that, all `makefile`-related variables (@MPICC@, @CFLAGS@, etc.) are adapted. Configure tries to detect or guess all of those variables. However, by supplementing this information on the command line in standard fashion,
`QUEUE=express MPI_VERSION=MPICH-ch_gm-1.2.5 ./configure; make; make run`
it is possible to override the detection. For the IPACS benchmark, this feature is especially useful, since it allows to run different benchmarks versions (implementation and device of MPI version, compile flags etc.) on the same platform by simply changing the environment variable in the IPACS GUI.

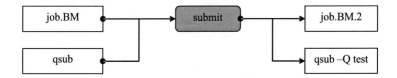

Figure 6.5: Final adaption of the batch script

6.2.2.4 Submit-Time Adaption of the Batch Script

The above variables, especially the batch script header, are batch system specific and replaced during build/configure time. Since the IPACS execution framework has to be able to submit several benchmark jobs into the queue (for all the processor numbers given in PROC_ARRAY); in addition, it is necessary to patch the batch script during submit time. The following variables are adapted by the submit script itself:

CF_TIME Walltime for the job. Usually depends on the number of processors currently allocated.

CF_NODE Number of nodes. Directly derived from number of processors.

CF_BENCH Name of benchmark.

CF_TCPU Number of processors.

CF_NCPU Number of procs per node: NODE_NUM_PROCS.

CF_PE Name of parallel environment queue.

For batch systems, which need specific command line flags for the submit, the actual submit command has to be patched in addition to the above variables. The final adaption of the script thus will have the structure as shown in Figure 6.5.

6.2.2.5 Runtime-Time Adaption of Machinefiles

Since some information is available only at runtime (the information, on which machines the job is going to run), we also need a runtime adaption. Fortunately there is only one such adaption needed and this is the machinefile. The mpirun in the IPACS framework is a generic wrapper, which just understands 2 flags, namely the number of processors and the application to run. This wrapper then calls a specific wrapper (determined during configure time), which knows how the machinefiles can be derived from the nodefile the batch system provides and how to run the mpirun command if such information is not required. In a final step, the original mpirun of the MPI implementation is called with all proper flags and a correct machinefile.

6.2.2.6   Example – TAUBENCH

```
#!/bin/sh
#
# christian.simmendinger@t-systems.com
#
# SYNOPSIS
#       job.TauBench
#
#@BL1@
#@BL2@
#@BL3@
#@BL4@
#@BL5@
#@BL6@
np=CF_TCPU
if test x"@CONFIGDIR@" != x"@SCRDIR@"; then
    cp @CONFIGDIR@/TauBench @SCRDIR@
fi
cd @SCRDIR@
@CONFIGDIR@/mpirun -np $np ./TauBench >& TauBench.p$np
cp TauBench.p$np @CONFIGDIR@/RESULTS
rm -f TauBench.p$np
```

Listing 6.1: Workflow of TAUBENCH– Generic Batch Script

```
#!/bin/sh
#
# christian.simmendinger@t-systems.com
#
# SYNOPSIS
#       job.TauBench
#
#PBS -l walltime=CF_TIME
#PBS -l nodes=CF_NODE
#PBS -N CF_BENCH
#
#
#
np=CF_TCPU
if test x"/cacau/hww/hwwadm4/ipacs/TauBench-1.2" != x"/cacau/
   hww/hwwadm4/ipacs/TauBench-1.2"; then
```

```
        cp /cacau/hww/hwwadm4/ipacs/TauBench-1.2/TauBench /cacau/
            hww/hwwadm4/ipacs/TauBench-1.2
fi
cd /cacau/hww/hwwadm4/ipacs/TauBench-1.2
/cacau/hww/hwwadm4/ipacs/TauBench-1.2/mpirun -np $np ./
    TauBench >& TauBench.p$np
cp TauBench.p$np /cacau/hww/hwwadm4/ipacs/TauBench-1.2/
    RESULTS
rm -f TauBench.p$np
```

Listing 6.2: Build-Time Adaption of the Batch Script

```
#!/bin/sh
#
# christian.simmendinger@t-systems.com
#
# SYNOPSIS
#      job.TauBench
#
#PBS -l walltime=2:00:00
#PBS -l nodes=2
#PBS -N TauBench
#
#
#
np=4
if test x"/cacau/hww/hwwadm4/ipacs/TauBench-1.2" != x"/cacau/
    hww/hwwadm4/ipacs/TauBench-1.2"; then
      cp /cacau/hww/hwwadm4/ipacs/TauBench-1.2/TauBench /cacau/
          hww/hwwadm4/ipacs/TauBench-1.2
fi
cd /cacau/hww/hwwadm4/ipacs/TauBench-1.2
/cacau/hww/hwwadm4/ipacs/TauBench-1.2/mpirun -np $np ./
    TauBench >& TauBench.p$np
cp TauBench.p$np /cacau/hww/hwwadm4/ipacs/TauBench-1.2/
    RESULTS
rm -f TauBench.p$np
```

Listing 6.3: Submit-Time Adaption of the Batch Script

6.2.2.7 Interaction with the IPACS Client

The execution framework above is autonomous and can be called independently from of
the IPACS client in order to allow a broader community to use this framework. The

IPACS client is responsible for the deployment of the benchmark sources. It also handles the retrieval of the benchmark results. The execution of the benchmark is handled by the above framework, which is called by the client in standard mode e.g:

```
PROC_ARRAY="2 4 8" QUEUE="parallel" SCRDIR="/tmp" ./configure; make; make
run
```

6.2.3   Outlook

In order to allow the Grid software stacks to make use of this tool and in order to support a wider range of HPC platforms for the IPACS project itself, we have made this part of the IPACS framework an independent SourceForge project.

Chapter 7

University of Rostock, Chair of Computer Architecture

7.1 I/O Benchmarking

Since the performance gap between main memory and secondary storage increases rapidly during the last years and the I/O performance is a known bottleneck in modern CPUs, the analysis of secondary storage performance becomes very important. With the increasing appearance of cluster computer and parallel network storage systems, the I/O benchmarking becomes more difficult.

Associative or content addressable memory has a great advantage in large environments. Grids are very dynamic and the storage of data by using the host addresses is not usable. To overcome this content addressable memory can be used. The location of a dataset is not defined by an address, but by a key, which can be the contents of the dataset, or only a part of that.

The next sections will describe the problems of getting useful benchmark results in a widely-spread hardware and software environment, a solution for a comprehensive I/O benchmark, the PRIOMARK, and a content addressable memory for computing grids.

7.2 I/O in Local and Distributed Systems

Modern computer systems use a hierarchical storage architecture, called memory hierarchy [57]. Typically, the memory hierarchy consists of CPU registers being the highest level, 1st level cache, 2nd level cache, main memory and disk storage. Each level of this hierarchy has a larger memory capacity and is slower than higher levels. The memory hierarchy aims at minimizing the latency of accesses to memory by caching frequently-used data in higher hierarchy levels. Using this technology minimizes the input and output of fast CPUs to slow memory hierarchy levels to produce a maximum data supply of the processor.

Figure 7.1 shows the hierarchy for a typical local computer system. Especially in distributed systems, the hierarchy can consist of additional levels, e. g. 3rd level cache

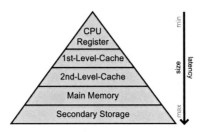

Figure 7.1: The memory hierarchy

or more mass-storage levels. I/O benchmarking covers the performance of data transfers between main memory and mass storage and is of special interest because the bandwidth of transmissions between these two levels is the slowest between all levels of the described hierarchy. Mostly I/O benchmarks are file system benchmarks. Benchmarks of this type measure the performance of accesses to files in file systems.

7.2.1 File Systems and File System Interfaces

Operating systems organize data storage in hierarchical structures, called file systems. Basically, file systems provide files and directories to the user. Files store the data itself and directories store information for organizing files in logical groups. Users are able to navigate through these structures and can access their data.

The main file access operations are `create`, `open`, `close`, `read`, `write` and `delete`. Any of these file system operations are done by an operating system call. This enables the operating system to optimize accesses to disk storage e. g. by caching disk storage date in main memory.

For accessing files, standardized file system interfaces that provide the necessary file access operations are used. The POSIX-I/O interface is common in most modern operating systems and is a well-known file system interface [58]. It was designed to support file systems on a local storage device.

POSIX-I/O had not been developed to allow parallel accesses to files from many nodes of a distributed computer system. To overcome this problem the message passing library specification, MPI-2 contains the file system interface MPI-IO [16]. This file system interface is optimized for concurrent accesses to a file system. As many processes can access one file concurrently, MPI-IO provides many different methods for synchronizing these accesses.

- *Individual file pointer* accesses allow every process to work on its own portion of the file. Every process has its own file pointer.

- *Shared file pointer* access methods allow all processes to work with one common file pointer. Concurrent accesses act as they are serialized, but the real disk I/O can be done in parallel.

- When using accesses with *explicit offset* a process specifies the position of every operation within the file.

Every described access method can be used in *blocking* or *non-blocking* and *collective* or *non-collective* mode.

- *Blocking I/O operations* will suspend the calling process as long as the operation did not complete, while *non-blocking operations* return immediately indicating a successful execution of the operation by the return value.

- *Collective I/O-calls* will be done by a group of processes. As all processes of the group access the file, there are many more possibilities of optimizing the accesses by the system than by using the *non-collective* counterparts of the functions.

Thus, there is a number of possibilities of accessing files in a file system by means of the MPI-IO interface. A distributed I/O benchmark has to take all these possibilities into consideration.

As file system benchmarks examine the performance of the complete file system calls, they also take caches of the other memory hierarchy levels into account. In order to avoid the disturbing effects of such caches, there are benchmarks that bypass the disk cache of the operating system. They are called disk I/O benchmarks. These benchmarks access disks directly or by means of a special device driver that is provided by the operating system. Thus, disk I/O benchmarks are often hardware or operating system dependent.

7.2.2   I/O Classification

Flynn's taxonomy of computer systems categorizes machines by the number of concurrent instruction and data streams [59]. It divides computer architectures into the classes:

- SISD – single instruction, single data stream,

- SIMD – single instruction, multiple data stream,

- MISD – multiple instruction, single data stream, and

- MIMD – multiple instruction, multiple data stream.

As stated in Section 7.1, the performance evaluation of I/O transfers to secondary storage is of special interest. Therefore, an I/O taxonomy is a useful method used to categorize I/O systems and I/O application behavior. Such a taxonomy must be generally applicable to workstations as well as high performance parallel computing systems. It gives an overview about existing architectures with their organizations and makes it possible to categorize new developments. The suggested I/O classification method is based

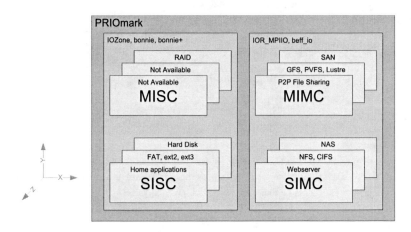

Figure 7.2: The I/O taxonomy with three dimensions

on Flynn's two-dimensional taxonomy and has further dimensions for the categorization of I/O systems and I/O behavior of applications.

Figure 7.2 shows the I/O taxonomy. Dimension X represents the number of clients (SC – *Single Client*, MC – *Multiple Client*) accessing I/O nodes. The number of I/O nodes is represented by dimension Y (SI – *Single I/O node*, MI – *Multiple I/O node*). In dimension Z three levels of use for the suggested taxonomy are shown. The 1st level categorizes I/O technologies or systems, while the 2nd level classifies file systems. In the 3rd level, application I/O behavior is ordered.

The 1st I/O category is *Single I/O node – Single Client* (SISC-I/O or simply SISC). It is the simplest form of I/O. One client is accessing one I/O node. A typical I/O technology of this category is a single hard disk in a workstation, where one CPU accesses the disk. Typical local file systems can be arranged in this category, e.g. the FAT file system and 2nd or 3rd extended file systems that are commonly used on Linux operating systems. SISC applications are single workstation applications like office programs.

Single I/O node – Multiple Client (SIMC-I/O or SIMC) is the 2nd category. It characterizes I/O where one I/O node is accessed by multiple clients. A Network Attached Storage (NAS) as storage technology allowing access of multiple clients to one I/O server is for example classified into this I/O technology class [60]. Commonly used SIMC file systems are NFS (Network File System) [21] or CIFS (Common Internet File System) [61]. Applications that reflect the described I/O behavior are all client-server-applications, e.g. web-server.

The category *Multiple I/O nodes – Single Client* (MISC-I/O or MISC) comprises I/O operations where multiple I/O nodes are used by a single client. That is the case for RAID as a storage system. It joins many hard disks for one system or CPU [62]. There are no MISC file systems, but some special MISC applications e.g. special database systems.

Access from many clients to many I/O nodes is named as *Multiple I/O nodes – Multiple Clients* (MIMC-I/O or MIMC). Storage Area Networks (SAN) are one storage technology belonging to this type of I/O. It connects many I/O nodes by a special interconnect network and supports storage for multiple clients [63]. Examples for MIMC-I/O file systems are GFS (Global File System) by RedHat [22] [23], PVFS (Parallel Virtual File System) [25] and Lustre by Cluster File Systems, Inc [24]. Any of these file systems support the distribution of data to many I/O nodes increasing the fault tolerance, performance and scalability of the file system. Peer-to-peer file sharing is an example for a MIMC application.

I/O benchmarks are special applications and therefor can be categorized by the I/O taxonomy, too. Well-known benchmarks like BONNIE [17] and IOZONE [18] use the POSIX-I/O file system interface commonly used in UNIX operating systems. These benchmarks normally use one client node to examine local file systems. Thus, they are SISC and MISC applications. A second kind of I/O benchmarks that is commonly used to examine I/O performance of network and distributed file systems, are benchmarks using file system interfaces for high performance I/O. Such a file system interface is MPI-IO defined in the MPI-2 specification [16]. Well known MPI-IO benchmarks are B_{eff_io} [19] and IOR_MPIIO [64]. Benchmarks that use this file system interface are called parallel I/O benchmarks. They use many concurrently running processes to access data. Those benchmarks are SIMC and MIMC applications.

All presented benchmarks have in common that they use one file system interface only and thus can be used either for single client I/O (SISC, MISC) or multiple client I/O (SIMC, MIMC). Since there was no benchmark examining all four described domains, we developed the PRIOMARK as an integrated I/O benchmark (see work-package description 2.2.3, for a detailed description of the PRIOMARK see Section 7.3). It is able to examine the I/O performance of applications of all described domains. The presented taxonomy shows one type of classifying different I/O access types. A more detailled workload classification is presented in the next section. It is the basis for defining benchmarks that supply most meaningful results for special applications.

7.2.3 Workload-based I/O Classification

I/O workloads describe the manner of how applications access secondary storage. These access patterns are characterized by order, size, position, type (read or write access) and number of serial or parallel accesses to the memory [65]. As I/O benchmarks are special applications they also use a defined I/O workload. This workload is of special importance when analyzing the measurement results of I/O benchmarks because it significantly affects the measured values. Section 7.3.2 presents measurements with different workloads to show the influence of different workload configurations on the benchmark results. The presented results clearly show that I/O benchmark results are representative for applications using an I/O workload comparable to the workload of the benchmark, only.

The following sections present types of I/O benchmarks differentiating between their workload and define a taxonomy of I/O benchmarks using these types.

7.2.3.1 Benchmarks with Defined Workload

Most available I/O benchmarks for local and distributed computing systems use workloads statically defined by the benchmark developer.

In the following, some of these benchmarks will be introduced briefly. One of the most common I/O benchmarks for local systems is BONNIE. It accesses sequentially arranged and randomly determined blocks of the mass storage. Four different processes are doing the coincidental accesses. They read one random block in a newly generated file and write it back in 10 percent of all cases [17].

A common I/O benchmark for distributed I/O systems is NAS BTIO. Contrary to other presented I/O benchmarks, this benchmark uses the MPI-IO file system interface. BTIO computes a matrix, which is written to the secondary storage each after five calculation steps. Thus, this benchmark uses one widespread I/O workload of parallel applications only, the so-called checkpoint write workload [66].

It is verified that many existing I/O benchmarks are using defined workloads for special problems. Thus, the obtained results are characteristic for special applications only and do not characterize the I/O performance of the system in general. In order to avoid this problem of the defined workloads, Chen and Patterson describe five different parameters for the characterization of I/O workload and a method, obtaining widely applicable benchmark results for I/O systems [65]. These five workload parameters are defined subsequently:

- **uniqueBytes** the total quantity of accessed data

- **sizeMean** the average size of an I/O requests

- **seqFrac** proportion of sequential accesses

- **readFrac** proportion of reading accesses

- **processNum** amount of concurrently accessing processes

These five parameters allow the specification of workloads for different applications. For an universal I/O benchmark, characterizing all possible conceivable applications, it is necessary to measure the complete five-dimensional workload space. As Chen and Patterson notice correctly, this procedure is extremely time-intensive and therefore not practicable. According to these authors, the measurement of the complete workload space of a Sprite DECstation would approximatly last two months. Therefore, they suggest a measuring method, calculating one graph per variable parameter with constant values for all further dimensions. The constant values for the other parameters are determined heuristically. It is noticeable that such a procedure represents only parts of the entire workload parameter space. Besides the difficult comparability of different benchmark results due to the variety of received data results, there is still the problem that results are only applicable for certain applications similarly as when using defined workloads. It still cannot be guaranteed that the determined results are characteristic for the application used on a system. Therefore, a possibility of categorizing existing I/O benchmarks on the basis of its used I/O measuring methods is presented. On the basis of this categorization it is stated, which measuring method supplies the best results for the user.

So far, it is stated that most existing benchmarks use defined workloads. Their disadvantages are clearly shown. The approach of Chen and Patterson measures larger parts of the workload space. Thus, the effort of time for the measurement rises. However, it is questionable whether the results are better applicable for different applications thereby. The approaches introduced in this paper assume users running few applications on the computing system only. In particular, this is the case when using cluster computers and other high performance computers, because, commonly, these are procured for specific applications. Since the I/O workload of an application corresponds to one point in the five-dimensional workload space, it is sufficient to only measure this appropriate point in order to achieve an optimal comparability of different systems when using this application. Therefore, three different approaches will be introduced in the following paragraphs.

7.2.3.2 Benchmarks with Configurable Workload

When using benchmarks with configurable workload, it is possible to specify the operating point within the five-dimensional I/O workload space. Thus, it is given the greatest possible flexibility. A user can adapt the benchmark to the exact conditions of an application, if he knows them. However, such a configurableness complicates the comparability of examined systems, since different users could use different parameters. Therefore, it is necessary to publicate the used workload with the publication of measurement results. Additionally, benchmark developers can provide pre-defined workloads with the distribution of their benchmark, in order to define standard configurations.

In the context of the IPACS project providing scalable and realistic benchmarks for distributed computer systems, we developed the PRIOMARK, an I/O benchmark with configurable workloads. Besides IOBENCH [67] and IOZONE [18], it is one of a few benchmarks of this type. PRIOMARK features a flexible configuration of I/O workloads and supplies several pre-defined workloads for different application fields (for example a web server workload, a workload for typical workstation I/O behavior and different workload definitions for parallel applications). Section 7.3 gives a detailed description of the PRIOMARK and its features.

A special problem of I/O benchmarks with configurable workloads is that the user must possess a good knowledge of the I/O behavior of the specific applications. Often, this is not the case. Therefore, there is the possibility of automating the procedure of workload configuration by analysis of the I/O behavior of the targeted application. This leads to application-based benchmarks.

7.2.3.3   Application-based Benchmarks

A goal of application-based benchmarks is the automated analysis of the I/O behavior of applications and the automatic production of a workload configuration, which corresponds to the result of this analysis. In particular, it is important to analyze applications, whose source code is not available. Depending upon application and operating system, there are different approaches for the realization of such an I/O profiler:

- logging of I/O calls in the operating system

- logging of I/O calls in the C library

- logging of MPI-IO calls of parallel applications in the MPI library

The first two approaches are applicable to all applications, which access the secondary storage directly using system calls of the operating system. Typically, this is the case with non-distributed applications. Using the 1st approach, it is necessary to change the operating system in a way that the typical I/O system calls are mapped onto own implementations, accomplishing a logging apart from the call of the original function. Operating system cores include a table containing pointers to functions of the individual system calls. A modification of the system calls is simply possible, as the pointers to functions in this table are changed in such a way that they point to the newly-implemented functions. However, for using this approach, the operating systems source code must be available, as it is the case with Linux.

The 2nd approach is applicable using operating systems, whose source code is not freely available, too. It implements a library, which is linked against the application instead of the standard C library of the operating system. The functions within this library are logging the calls during their execution. Both described solutions for the implementation of an I/O profiler are only conditionally applicable to distributed I/O systems, which use the MPI-IO interface. On the one hand, such systems implement the access to the distributed memory system commonly using a user space library. This library accomplishes the data transfer not using the local file system interface, but using the network interface connected to the regarded I/O node. Therefore, all methods, which log accesses to the local secondary storage interface, do not work properly in this case. On the other hand, logging the local I/O system calls leads to a loss of information since the MPI-IO interface is very complex. There are a lot of different MPI-IO access methods that can lead to different accesses to the storage even depending on the used file system. Thus, the 3rd presented approach for implementing an I/O profiler is implemented in the same way as the 2nd proposal but uses a wrapper for the MPI-IO library instead of the standard C library.

The three presented solutions for the implementation of an I/O profiler lead to the problem that the added code portions produce additional load and thereby affect the total performance of the examined applications negatively. However, the additional func-

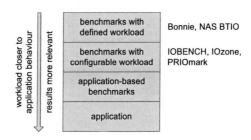

Figure 7.3: Workload-based I/O classification

tionality does not influence the I/O behavior of the application. Thus, the logged data is always correct. It can also be processed correctly by the benchmark.

Benchmarks, which use the logged I/O workload of generic applications, produce comparable results that reflect the real I/O workload behavior of an application. Therefore, another goal of the IPACS project was implementing an extension module for the PRIOMARK, which permits such possibilities for Linux applications (see Section 7.3.1.5).

7.2.3.4 Applications as Benchmarks

Measurement results corresponding best to the real application performance, can be obtained while integrating the performance measurement into application. For example, there are some applications containing methods for measuring the frame rate for sequences of pictures in order to be able to estimate the graphical performance of the application on different hardware. There are also some programs determining the I/O performance of data transfers between computing systems, such as some FTP clients. Such an integration of the performance measurement into existing programs has to be implemented by the application programmer and is in particular uncommon with larger applications.

7.2.3.5 Classification of Measurement Techniques

Figure 7.3 shows the presented workload-based I/O measuring methods and benchmarks using these methods. Benchmark results are more relevant the more their behavior corresponds to that of the application to be executed on the system. The performance measurement within the application corresponds most to the relevant performance results attainable by the application. As described in Section 7.2.3.1, the relevance of results of synthetic benchmarks with defined workloads is to be regarded as problematic, while benchmarks described in Section 7.2.3.2 are able to supply meaningful results when using a suitable configuration.

Thus, these benchmarks with configurable workload measure only one point of the five-dimensional workload space, which should correspond to the application as exactly as possible. In order to support the user in the determination of a relevant benchmark configuration, I/O profilers can be used. If the output of I/O profilers are processed by a benchmark program, benchmarks are generated, whose results can be consulted best for a comparison of different systems. They are called application-based benchmarks. Applications, which contain even benchmark methods, are rather rarely and in practice also less relevant, since such an integration has to be implemented by the application programmer.

To implement an I/O benchmark that describes the performance of applications best we developed the PRIOMARK, a configurable and application-based I/O benchmark. The architecture and features of the PRIOMARKare presented subsequently.

7.3   The PRIOMARK

The PRIOMARK is a novel I/O benchmark for local and distributed computing systems. It implements a variety of sub-benchmarks for measuring different access methods and I/O interfaces. Furthermore, it is extensible and easy to use. The PRIOMARK enhances available disk performance measurement programs by the following features:

- support of POSIX-I/O and MPI-IO file system interfaces,

- a complex workload definition for all implemented sub-benchmarks,

- even POSIX-I/O interface benchmarks are available in distributed environments,

- an asynchronous MPI-IO and POSIX-I/O benchmark,

- a disk I/O benchmark (raw disk I/O),

- a meta operation benchmark,

- a single value as benchmark result for an easy comparison,

- and a plug-in architecture to integrate extended sub-benchmarks.

The next sections will describe the necessity and the implementation of the PRIOMARK and its enhancements in comparison to available I/O benchmarks.

7.3.1   Concept and Implementation

The next sections describe the concept and architecture of the PRIOMARK. This includes an overview about implemented sub-benchmarks, the possibilities of defining complex workloads and the usage in non-parallel environments. For implementing the PRIOMARKwe first developed a benchmark framework assisting the user in implementing benchmarks especially for measuring I/O performance. This benchmark framework is the basis for the PRIOMARKand is explained in the following section.

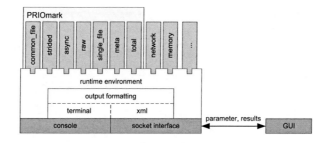

Figure 7.4: Benchmark Framework

7.3.1.1 Benchmark Framework

The developed framework for building benchmark suites is plugin-based. Benchmarks can easily and dynamically integrated as single plugins. This offers an easy building of a special benchmark suite with chosen benchmark plugins.

In Figure 7.4, the framework and its components are shown. The *runtime environment* administrates the installed benchmark plugins. In the picture, they are illustrated as plugs in the upper part. Configurable variables and its default values are stored in a data structure of every plugin. In order to change the default values for a benchmark run, the user may write a new configuration file which is analyzed by the *runtime environment* while starting the benchmark suite. Then, it executes the selected benchmark plugins. A *framework library*, also being part of the *runtime environment*, provides common functions for the plugins, e.g. functions for time measurement and statistical evaluation.

The results of all benchmark plugins are collected, formatted and written to the configured output device by the *output formatting module*. It is also extensible and up to now, two output plugins were implemented. The *terminal-plugin* writes the results as text to the standard output stream, while the *XML-plugin* generates a XML-document. This document can either be written to standard output or a server provides it over a network connection. The output formatting module supports structured output of text, single values, linear equations, and tables with two or three dependent values generated by the benchmark plugins. The XML output provided by a network connection is used by a *graphical user interface client*. It is implemented in the Java programming language and thus platform-independent. In the *GUI* the configuration data is editable in a user-friendly way and, as in the console version, the executed benchmark plugins are selectable. The measurement results are presented graphically. Figure 7.5 shows a screen-shot of the GUI-client with results from a small disk benchmark.

The *runtime environment* supports a stand-alone execution with only one process as well as a parallel run with many concurrent processes. MPI message passing is used for the communication between the processes in the parallel variant and the result data generated by the single processes is collected and presented by the first MPI process

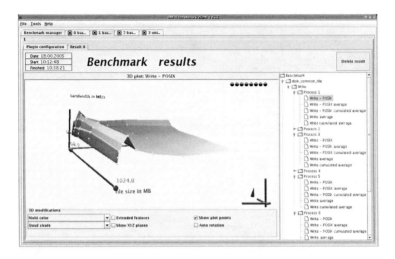

Figure 7.5: Benchmark Framework GUI

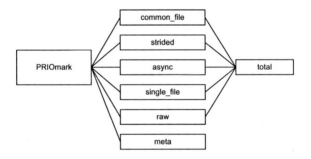

Figure 7.6: PRIOMARK benchmark plugins

(MPI root process). Within the *output formatting module* of this process, the measured results can be post-processed to calculate benchmark averages, linear regressions or other statistical values.

7.3.1.2   PRIOMARK **Benchmark Plugins**

The PRIOMARK is a special benchmark application using the framework mentioned above. It comprises of different benchmark plugins (sub-benchmarks) for I/O measurement.

As shown in Figure 7.6, the sub-benchmarks common_file, strided, async, single_file, raw, and meta are included. The last plug-in total calculates one single value out of the results of the previously mentioned sub-benchmarks (with the exception of the `meta` benchmark). Those will be described in the following paragraphs.

common_file

This sub-benchmark acquires bandwidths for block-by-block accesses of a huge amount of processes to a single file. Each process is represented by one consecutive data block within the file (see Figure 7.7.a). The file size and the size for an I/O request varies. The following access patterns are tested:

- *Write*: creating and filling a new file with the specified file size,

- *Read/Write*: reading and re-writing of an existing file, and

- *Random Read/Write*: reading and re-writing of randomly chosen blocks in an existing file.

For *read/write* and *random read/write* accesses the ratio between read and write operations can be defined freely (see Section 7.3.1.3). All measurements can use the collective and non-collective blocking MPI-IO access methods *individual file pointer* and *explicit offset*. As the MPI-IO interface is not available in all MPI implementations, measurements use POSIX-I/O functions, too.

strided

This benchmark uses MPI file views to measure the I/O performance of accesses from many processes to a single file. Contrary to the `common_file` test, every process has a defined count of non-consecutive data blocks (see Figure 7.7.b). It tests the access patterns *write* and *read/write* (with the same semantics as for `common_file`). The number of continuous blocks of one stride as well as the file and block sizes can be defined freely. For *read/write* accesses the read-write-ratio can also be specified by the user. This benchmark uses the MPI-IO *individual file pointers* for data access only.

async

Asynchronous I/O is very important for high performance computing applications. It allows reading or writing data and still being able to calculate new information. Concurrent data transfers and computing increases the load of the bus system. Due to this fact the performance of the concurrently executed operations is lower as in the case where both were serialized. Therefore, the async benchmark measures the asynchronous calculation loss (ACL) and the asynchronous bandwidth loss (ABL) of the parallel operations in relation to the serialized operations. The test uses the read/write access pattern with MPI-IO *individual file pointer, explicit offset* and POSIX-I/O access methods.

single_file

This test is designed to measure the bandwidth of block-by-block accesses to the local disk. It only uses the POSIX-I/O interface. Contrary to the POSIX-I/O benchmarks

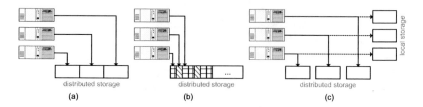

Figure 7.7: PRIOMARK benchmark access modes

introduced in Section 7.2.3, processes using this benchmark can also be distributed. In that case every process has its own test file. Figure 7.7.c presents the available storage access modes. In addition to the access patterns *write*, *read/write* and *random read/write*, this benchmark supports a *backwards read* test. This means that the test file is read block-by-block in reversed order. File size and block size can be defined freely, as well as the ratio between read and write accesses for *read/write* and *random read/write* access patterns.

meta

Meta operations are necessary file management operations, e. g. creating and deleting files or directories. Up to now, the `meta` sub-benchmark supports the performance measurement of three meta operation combinations from the POSIX-I/O file system interface:

1. **fopen − fclose**: open and close an existing file

2. **open − close**: open and close an existing file

3. **creat − close − unlink**: create and open a new file, close and delete it

The benchmark measures each of this combinations in a loop for a user defined time and calculates an average in operations per second.

raw

Unlike the other tests, this sub-benchmark is not a file system but a disk I/O benchmark. It measures the performance of raw-disk accesses to the local secondary storage. This allows measuring the true speed of the storage because raw-devices do not use operating system buffer caches. The bandwidth is measured by the access patterns *read/write* and *random read/write*. As for all other tests the read-write-ratio can be specified together with the data size and the block size (which must be multiples of the raw disk block size).

total

Because of the detailed output of the different sub-benchmarks `total` can be used to collect all their values and calculates an average (with except of the `meta` sub-benchmark which does not measure a bandwidth). This value guarantees an easy comparison of the I/O performance of many different systems.

When running the PRIOMARK, the user can specify which of the tests common_file, strided, async, single_file, raw, and meta should be executed. This allows to run dedicated benchmarks for local storage access (raw, single_file, meta), distributed file access (common_file, strided, async) or mixed accesses.

7.3.1.3 The Workload Definition

The PRIOMARK benchmark supports processing of a complex application-specific workload definition. For all sub-benchmarks with exception of the async and the meta test, the user may specify a range of file/data sizes and a range of block sizes for a single I/O request. For the access patterns *read/write* and *random read/write*, the user may select the ratio between read and write requests. If a sub-benchmark supports different access methods (POSIX-I/O, MPI-IO *individual file pointer*, ...) the methods to be chosen are a matter of configuration, too. For the async sub-benchmark the user may choose the expected data size only, because this test has to read or write the whole data in a single request. The configuration of the meta benchmark only supports the definition of the loop-time.

To all sub-benchmarks applies that if more than one measurement method (e. g. *write*, *read/write*, *open – close*) is supported, the user can specify if all or only selected methods should be used.

The whole configuration is stored in a single file. Thus, it becomes easy to repeat the benchmark using the same settings. It is possible to store workloads for different application domains in separate files.

7.3.1.4 Parallel or Non-Parallel

As described in Section 7.3.1.1, at compile time, the user may choose whether he wants to build a parallel version of PRIOMARK able to run on distributed systems or a non-parallel version for single workstations. However, the sub-benchmarks common_file and strided are not available in the non-parallel version as they depend on MPI.

Additionally, it is possible to build a parallel benchmark without using the MPI-IO interface, because it is not available in every MPI implementation. That version uses the MPI communication interface for synchronizing the single processes and collecting the measured values. Thus, it is possible to acquire the I/O performance of many machines when applying the local storage test concurrently using a single benchmark run only.

7.3.1.5 I/O Profiler

As described in Section 7.2.3 the performed workload of a benchmark has an important influence on the reached results. Measurement results are more useful the better the benchmark workload imitates the applications I/O behaviour. Hence using applications

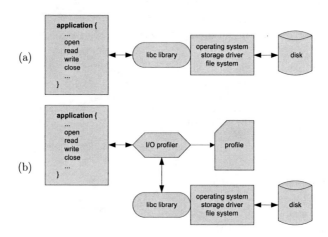

Figure 7.8: I/O profiling process

itself for benchmarking allows to draw the most useful conclusions about achievable performance of a system, but measurement functions have to be included in the applications. Therefor the collaboration of the software developer is necessary.

The Section 7.2.3.3 describes a benchmark method for getting application relevant results by using workloads of a real application. Thereto all I/O access calls of a program are logged and can be replayed by a special benchmark. In the referenced section there are described three different approaches for such an I/O profiler. For this project a C library I/O profiler (second approach) is implemented. This wrapper library provides all I/O functions for the applications and writes all storage accesses during their execution to a file. Figure 7.8 shows the usage of the profiler library. Part (a) of the picture abstractly shows the normal invoke of an I/O call, whereas in part (b) the profiler library is used.

Logged I/O accesses (with the various access calls of the POSIX-I/O interface) in the profile are:

- file / directory create, open, close, delete,

- seek within files, and

- read and write from / to files.

For each entry in the profile the time and the id of the calling process is stored. Data access calls are logged with a reference to the accessed file, the position within the file, and the size of the accessed data.

For replaying recorded profiles a benchmark plugin for the PRIOMARK is implemented. At first this sub-benchmark analyzes the profile file. With the above described informations in the profile, the plugin creates and fills the necessary data files for the

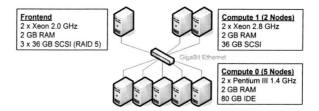

Figure 7.9: Cluster configuration

benchmark. After this step the benchmark starts replaying the profile and measures the elapsed time.

7.3.2   Measured Results

This section presents some benchmark results acquired by the PRIOMARK using a test system with different system configurations (parallel and non-parallel), file systems, and file system interfaces.

7.3.2.1   Test System

The test system for the measurements is a Linux cluster with the Rocks Linux 3.3.0 [68] and MPICH 1.2.6 [69] with ROMIO 1.2.5 [70] as parallel programming environment. ROMIO is compiled with support for NFS and PVFS and general support for all Unix like file systems (UFS). It consists of one frontend and seven compute nodes. The frontend node contains a dual processor 2 GHz Intel Xeon processor with 2 GB RAM and a three disk SCSI RAID 5 storage array. Five of the compute nodes are 1.4 GHz Pentium III dual processor systems with 1 GB RAM and a single IDE hard disk. The other two nodes are dual 2.8 GHz Xeon processor based systems with 2 GB RAM and a single SCSI hard disk. All nodes are connected by Gigabit Ethernet. Figure 7.9 shows the cluster setup.

For the tests, different file systems are installed. Disk partitions for local storage are formatted with the very common Linux 3rd extended file system (*ext3*) [71]. Used file systems for distributed storage are *NFS*, *GFS*, *PVFS*, and *Lustre*.

NFS – Network File System

The Network File System as SIMC file system is the most common system to provide data over networks. It uses a central server for data storage [21]. Due to this fact, the server represents a bottleneck and single-point-of-failure. For the measurements the *Frontend* node exports a disk partition via NFS to the cluster nodes. The used disk partition on the Frontend is formatted with a 3rd extended file system.

GFS – Global File System

The Global File System developed by RedHat is a scalable alternative to NFS. As MIMC file system, it allows configurations avoiding single-point-of-failures because every component can be instantiated more than once. This file system is laid out to scale much better than NFS [22] [23]. The GFS is configured as following: Nodes of type *Compute 1* export a whole disk partition to all nodes via GNBD (Global Network Block Device). These partitions are bound together by a stripe size of 1 MB and formatted as GFS volume. Furthermore, the *Frontend* node and the nodes of type *Compute 1* act as lock server and the *Compute 0* nodes mount the file system.

PVFS – Parallel Virtual File System

The Parallel Virtual File System is designed to optimize concurrent access of many processes to the file system. Like other MIMC file systems, it distributes one file to a number of I/O nodes. Moreover, a metadata server provides the information about which node contains what part of a file. Hence, this server is a single-point-of-failure [25]. PVFS is designed to provide scratch space for large distributed applications. For the tests PVFS version 1.6.0 is used and configured as follows: The nodes of type *Compute 1* act as I/O server and export a chunk of their disk space, which is bound together using a stripe size of 64 KB. The *Frontend* node is the necessary metadata server, while all compute nodes act as PVFS clients and mount the file system.

Lustre

This MIMC file system is developed and maintained by Cluster File Systems, Inc. as a storage architecture for large clusters. It consists of Object Storage Targets (OST) providing file I/O service, Meta Data Server (MDS) storing file information, and clients. Lustre allows to setup every component more than once to improve reliability and throughput. The open source release Lustre Lite (Lustre 1.0.4) used in our environment has no load balancing capabilities while accessing meta-data services [24]. In the configuration used, the *Compute 1* nodes act as OST's and provide a chunk of their disk space, which are bound together using a stripe size of 1 MB. Furthermore, one *Compute 1* node acts as a MDS and the *Compute 0* nodes mount the file system.

7.3.2.2 Parallel Benchmarks

For evaluating the I/O performance of the test configurations for the distributed file systems *NFS*, *GFS*, *PVFS*, and *Lustre*, the sub-benchmark `common_file` is performed using two different workloads, a *checkpoint* and a *parallel application* scenario. The *checkpoint* scenario is characterized by pure reading of data, which happens when restoring application processes to a specific checkpoint state. Data is read by all processes from a common file. In the *parallel application* scenario, all processes read data from and write data to a common file. The ratio between read and write accesses is set to 1. All scenarios have a data size of 2 GB per process with an I/O request size of 4 MB. Using this big I/O

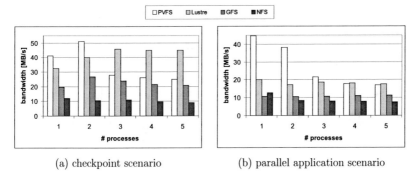

(a) checkpoint scenario   (b) parallel application scenario

Figure 7.10: PRIOMARK parallel workload comparison measurement results

requests is a core statement from [72], which says that in parallel applications, almost all I/O data is transferred by large requests. Every process has its own data block within the file and the I/O access methods POSIX-I/O and MPI-IO are measured. The reported bandwidths are the accumulated bandwidths of all concurrently running processes.

Figure 7.10.a shows the measured values for the *checkpoint* workload. When increasing the number of concurrent processes the *Lustre* bandwidth increases and reaches a stable value, whereas the *NFS* bandwidth decreases continuously. After reaching their maximum I/O performance at two concurrently running processes, the bandwidth of *PVFS* and *GFS* decreases continuously, too.

In Figure 7.10.b, the measurement results for the *parallel application* workload are presented. Under conditions of this workload and less than four concurrent processes *PVFS* reaches the best values. For more than three processes *PVFS* is slightly slower than *Lustre*, which reaches together with *GFS* for all process numbers an approximately constant bandwidth. Similar to the *checkpoint* workload the *NFS* bandwidth falls continuously.

Altogether, *Lustre* and *PVFS* are a good choice when running applications with concurrent file system access from many processes, because they are especially designed for parallel environments. Furthermore, it turns out that, even in case *PVFS*, *Lustre* and *GFS* are configured using two I/O nodes, *Lustre* and *PVFS* reach a better bandwidth. As expected, *NFS* with its single server concept is the slowest system in this comparison. The measurements also shows that the workload influences the file system performance strongly. This particularly applies to environments with concurrently running processes.

With the PRIOMARK it is possible to compare the performance of different file system interfaces and interface calls. As an example, measurements with the `common_file` subbenchmark on an *NFS* file system using the POSIX-I/O interface calls and the MPI-IO interface calls in its different variants (*individual file pointer*, *individual file pointer collective*, *explicit offset*, and *explicit offset collective*) and different process counts are done.

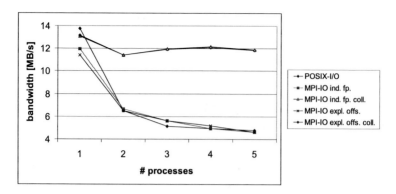

Figure 7.11: PRIOMARK file system interface comparison measurement results

The examined workload was already described and is the *parallel application* workload with a ration of 1 between read and write accesses and a data size per process of 2 GB with an I/O request size of 4 MB. The measured values are shown in Figure 7.11.

As one can see, collective MPI-IO file system calls reach a more than two times higher performance than noncollective MPI-IO or POSIX-I/O calls for more than two processes. The bandwidths of all file system calls are approximately similar if using only one processes. As described in Section 7.2.1, the MPI library optimizes concurrent disk access of many processes using collective I/O calls in order to achieve a higher bandwidth.

A comparison of using different counts of I/O nodes is shown in Figure 7.12. It shows the behavior of the *PVFS* file system. For this measurement, the number of concurrently running processes is set to 10 and nodes of type *Compute 0* of the described test cluster. Contrary to the *PVFS* setup described in Section 7.3.2.1 the *Compute 0* nodes are used as I/O nodes. The plot shows accumulated bandwidths and an approximately linear scaling behavior of the bandwidth when increasing the number of *PVFS* I/O nodes. This was to be expected, because *PVFS* distributes files to all I/O nodes. Therefore, it increases the accumulated bandwidth by adding new nodes.

7.3.2.3   Local Benchmarks

The average measurement results of the `single_file` sub-benchmark in dependency to the number of concurrently running processes on one compute node of type Compute 0 is shown in Figure 7.13. The benchmark is configured with the following parameters: file size 256 MB, block size 32 KB and read/write ratio 1/1 for test patterns *read/write* and *random read/write*.

As one can see, if the accumulated data size is smaller than the system's RAM (one to three concurrently running processes) the buffer cache of the operating system guarantees

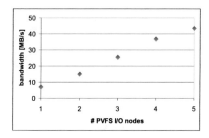

Figure 7.12: PRIOMARK measurement results with increasing counts of *PVFS* I/O nodes

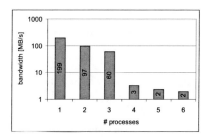

Figure 7.13: PRIOMARK measurement results of the `single_file` sub-benchmark

good performance. For more than three processes, the data size exceeds the 1 GB RAM of the system. Hence, there is a bandwidth break-in.

Figure 7.14 shows the average measured bandwidth from the `raw` sub-benchmark in dependence to data and block size on one compute node of type *Compute 0*. The ratio between read and write accesses for the *read/write* and *random read/write* tests is set to 1/0.

The chart shows, that the raw performance of the used disks is about 15 MB/s for small and 35 MB/s for large I/O requests. There is a maximum available bandwidth of more than 40 MB/s between an I/O request size of 64 KB and 256 KB. The examined data sizes show that the available transfer speed is independent of the system's RAM.

The presented results show clearly the advantages and features of the PRIOMARKcompared to other existing I/O benchmarks. The Chair of Computer Architecture also used the experience gathered by the development of PRIOMARKin developing a novel storage system based on a content addressable network. This CAN system and its improvements are presented subsequently.

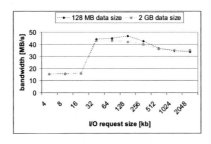

Figure 7.14: PRIOMARK measurement results of the raw sub-benchmark

7.4   Content Addressable Memory

Centralized network file systems like NFS are state-of-the-art in distributed computing with well-known drawbacks in availability and scalability. A central file system server provides a single point of failure for the whole system and a bottleneck preventing the system from being scalable [20]. In the area of cluster computing, these drawbacks have been largely overcome by distributed storage systems like Storage Area Networks and storage frameworks. One of these storage frameworks is Lustre, a commercial product by Cluster File Systems, Inc. [73]. These solutions distribute data among many I/O nodes and provide a more scalable and fault-tolerant system than centralized storage solutions. However, these systems require a central administration authority to control replication and data distribution and thus, are not usable in environments like computational grids [74].

Currently, there is no distributed data management system for computational grids that provides transparent data distribution and replication. There have been attempts for replica management in grid environments by the European Data Grid project resulting in Report [75], which still relies on a centralized metadata service.

Especially the storage and distribution of metadata for data management is a big problem in large storage systems. Metadata has to be updated on changes and is accessed by many hosts in parallel. Thus, often it is a bottleneck of the system. Eliminating the central metadata server can solve the described problems and is a goal of many modern peer-to-peer systems.

The utilization of research in the area of peer-to-peer computing is a possibility for effectively distributed data and replication management in environments without central administration authority. Thus, peer-to-peer systems seem to provide valuable algorithms and methods for data storage solutions in grid environments.

7.4.1 Algorithms from the Area of Peer-to-Peer Computing

The first generation of peer-to-peer systems like the well known file-sharing service Napster [76] uses one central database server that contains network addresses of nodes storing the information itself. Like other centralized data storage solutions, this generation of peer-to-peer systems is based on one central bottleneck and therefore, is not scalable. Thus, it is not usable in environments with a large number of storage nodes.

The next generation of peer-to-peer algorithms used for example in the Gnutella network [77] are "random power law graphs" (RPLGs). These algorithms operate completely without control over data distribution and replication. Therefore, they have no central authority which makes them very scalable. Searching in RPLGs is done by flooding all available parts of the storage network with requests. This results in exceeded network traffic and high latencies. Because of the high latencies and since controlled data distribution and replication in RPLGs is not possible, such algorithms are not useful in grid environments either.

Approaches that overcome these disadvantages are algorithms that base on "distributed hash tables" (DHT) like Chord and Pastry. Both organize the participating hosts in a logical ring using a sophisticated routing of messages. Detailed information on these algorithms can be found in [78] and [79]. A DHT that organizes hosts in a multi-dimensional structure is the Content-Addressable Network (CAN) that has been introduced by Ratnasamy et al in 2003 [80]. CAN will be briefly explained in the following after some words about its underlying principles.

Advantages of Content Addressable Memory

One problem in grid-based environments arises from the dynamic pool of nodes, which changes very much over time. This complicates maintaining a fixed address space very much. One way to overcome this problem is provided by the principle of content addressable memory.

Herein, the location of a dataset is not defined by an address but by a key value which is based on the contents of the dataset itself. This key can be the contents of the dataset itself or only a part of these contents. Thus, a dataset consists at least of a key and possibly of other data somehow connected to this key. This can for example be a file with the filename being the key as used in peer-to-peer file sharing applications.

The most common way to implement content addressable memory in software is the usage of hash functions, which map key values into a well-defined, uniformly distributed hash space. The values in hash space can now be mapped onto a fixed addressing scheme very easily. Since this procedure generates the same problem, as content addressable memory tried to solve in this context, distributed hash tables follow a different approach.

7.4.2   The Content Addressable Network

As mentioned before, data distribution with DHT based algorithms uses a hash function to map keys onto hash values, which can be evenly distributed over all participating nodes. Unlike the approach mentioned above, this distributed hash space is used as a basis for an overlay routing algorithm which makes it possible for every node to reach the one node that manages the inquired dataset.

7.4.2.1   The CAN Algorithm

The basis for CAN is a hash function that maps the key space onto a d-dimensional hash space. The hash space is divided among all nodes whereas every node knows its piece of the hash space, subsequently referred to as a zone. Furthermore, every node stores the network addresses of all its neighbors within the hash space. In order to reach the node storing a certain dataset, a node locates the dataset inside the hash space by calculating the hash value from the key to be searched for. Thereafter, it routes the query to one of its neighbors lessening the distance between the routing node and the node that contains the dataset with every routing step. The dataset is thereby reached on many different routing paths selectable by different characteristics. Figure 7.15 exemplarily shows a two-dimensional hash space with an overlay routing path.

The primary functionality of DHT-based algorithms like CAN includes the following operations:

Join - the inclusion of an additional node into the distributed storage system,

Leave - the removal of a node,

Store - the insertion of a dataset into the distributed memory,

Lookup - the retrieval of a dataset that fits a given key, and

Remove - the removal of a dataset from the system.

Moreover, CAN provides means of automatic, save and decentralized data replication. An important function that DHT-based algorithms cannot provide due to their foundation on hash functions is:

Query - the location of all datasets with their keys matching a given pair of key and mask.

An algorithm to be used as basis for distributed data storage systems in grids could benefit from this functionality, especially if the key information consists of structured data like for example IP-addresses, ISBNs or account numbers. There are different proposals in order to realize this functionality by using a second distributed storage network like CAN for special information about partial keys [81]. In the context of the IPACS project, we developed an algorithm to provide the query functionality using a single CAN.

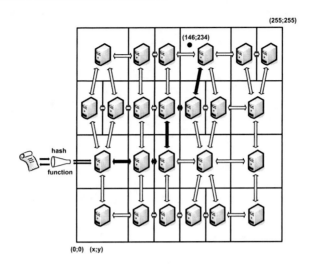

Figure 7.15: Inserting a document into a CAN-like managed key space:
Every node knows its neighbors as illustrated by the arrows. The documents key is
transformed into a two-dimensional hash value (in this case 146;234) and will be managed
by the node responsible for that part of the overall hash space. Thus, the node where the
document is inserted into the CAN must transfer it according to the CAN-routing which
in this example is illustrated by the dark arrows.

Additionally, there is a weakness to DHT-based algorithms founded on the usage of
overlay routing. Since routing inside the hash space is different from the underlying network routing, additional latencies are introduced. Research on this problem mainly goes
into one direction: Reduction of the number of overall routing steps from the searching
node to the one that manages the dataset to be located. A number of newer algorithms
have been introduced, which reduce the theoretical maximum number of routing steps.
Chord [78], Pastry [79] and Distance-Halving [82] are examples of these. While providing
a better theoretical routing performance they give up much of the flexibility and simplic-
ity of CAN. We have introduced an enhancement to CAN that does not only reduce the
average number of routing steps, but also enhances the algorithm by better exploiting
locality. Hence, the overlay routing draws nearer to the underlying network routing.

A third problem of data distribution across nodes using DHT-based algorithms is the
division of the hash space into zones that are each managed by one node. If the distributed
memory reaches a fill level of 50% and a node needs to be removed from the system or
runs out of storage space, it needs to dispense its zone or share it with another node. If
no new node is inserted into the system at this point it becomes impossible to re-merge
the zone with a neighbor because all these nodes do not have enough free storage space.

The whole system becomes very inflexible. We introduced a proposal to overcome this weakness.

7.4.2.2   Enhancements to the CAN Algorithm

As described before, we chose CAN as basis for our distributed storage algorithm because of its enormous flexibility. In the following paragraphs we describe three methods of enhancements to overcome the above-mentioned issues of CAN and DHTs. The first one introduces an algorithm to answer multiple data queries using one CAN. The next enhancement reduces the latencies triggered by differences between the overlay routing of CAN and the underlying IP-routing. The third improvement introduces multiple zones per node to overcome the inflexibility of storage networks with a fill-level of more than 50%.

Multiple Data Queries

The first enhancement of CAN that we developed is an implementation of the operation query mentioned above. We will therefore define the basic terms. Subsequently, a mask m that masks the differences between two keys k_1 and k_2 is defined as the exclusive disjunction of both keys: $m = k_1 \oplus k_2$. A query q is defined as a function of key k and mask m: $q(k, m)$. The results of a query can be defined as all keys k_i that match the equation:

$$k_i \in q(k, m) \Leftrightarrow (k \oplus k_i) \vee m = m \tag{7.1}$$

The basis for our enhancement is the choice of special hash functions. There is one major claim to hash functions in DHTs:

Data needs to be distributed equally across all participating storage nodes.

This is possible by equally distributing the keys over hash space assuming that the datasets are equally sized in average. We shall define another claim to our hash functions: They have to be traceable.

This means for a given hash function $f(x)$, any mask m, any key k and any key k' that

$$\text{if} \quad k' \in q(k, m) \quad \Rightarrow \quad f(k') \in q(f(k), f(m)) \quad \text{and} \tag{7.2}$$
$$\text{if} \quad f(k') \notin q(f(k), f(m)) \quad \Rightarrow \quad k' \notin q(k, m). \tag{7.3}$$

The simplest way to create such a hash function is to exchange bits inside of a key. Of course, extended knowledge about the predicted distribution of keys over the key space is fundamental to create a hash function that also fulfills claim (A).

Using a traceable hash function one can transform any query $q(k, m)$ into hash space. The transformed query $q(f(k), f(m))$ can be executed inside the hash space leading to the smallest possible result set that completely answers the query. This generates the same result set as if every possible key matching the query would have been transformed to hash space and searched for individually.

To answer a query inside the CAN we defined a recursive algorithm to route one query to all nodes, that manage relevant zones inside the hash space. A zone, as shown in Figure 7.15 before, can be defined by two values: One single hash value $f(k)$ belonging to this zone and a zone mask z. Now every hash value $f(k')$ is located inside the zone if and only if

$$f(k') \wedge z = f(k) \wedge z. \tag{7.4}$$

Our Algorithm can be described by the following three steps:

1. Given a mask m and a key k, the querying node calculates $f(m)$ and $f(k)$, puts them into its query and routes this query to the node managing $f(k)$.

2. The receiving node answers the query with all relevant result sets it stores. Additionally, it forwards the query according to the algorithm described by Listing 7.1. Therein the variable `bit` is used to mark the position of the bit inside `mask` and `key` which is currently processed by the algorithm. An example can be seen in Figure 7.16.

```
1    unsigned mask = f(m);
2    unsigned key = f(k);
3    unsigned zone = ~z;
4    unsigned bit = 0x80000000;
5    while ( bit > zone )
6    {
7        while ( bit > mask )
8            bit >>= 1;
9        mask ^= bit;
10       key ^= bit;
11       forward(key, mask);
12       key ^= b;
13   }
```

Listing 7.1: The forwarding algorithm for each node receiving a query. In line 11, the query is forwarded with the given values for key and mask.

3. Every node receiving the forwarded queries starts again at (2).

As one can see, in every loop of the algorithm, the number of bits set to 1 in $f(m)$ decreases by one (line 9) while the query is forwarded once (line 11). This stops as soon as there are no more bits set to 1 in $f(m)$ or the remaining bits do not change a keys value the way that it would be managed by another node (line 5).

To show that the algorithm forwards a query to the exact number of nodes, which could manage relevant hash values, we defined a forwarding level v and the sum of digits of the hash masks s_v. For the original query, we assume $v = 0$ because it was not yet processed and s_0 depicts the number of bits set to 1 in $f(m)$. After the first loop of the algorithm, the number of bits in $f(m)$ decreases by one and the query is forwarded once. This new query now has a forwarding level of $v = 1$ and its sum of digits $s_1 = s_0 - 1$. Ignoring the zone mask, the algorithm will loop until $f(m)$ has all bits set to 0 counting s_0 loops.

This means that the first node will forward s_0 queries with forwarding levels $v = 1 \ldots s_0$. There is one node receiving the query with $v = 1$. This node forwards s_1 queries with levels $v = 2 \ldots s_0$. So there are two nodes receiving queries with $v = 2$ and sending them with levels $v = 3 \ldots s_0$ and so on. An example of this behavior with the algorithm forwarding a certain query is pictured in Figure 7.17.

The maximum number of forwards F ignoring the zone mask can be calculated as:

$$F = s_0 + 2^0 s_1 + 2^1 s_2 + 2^2 s_3 + \ldots + 2^{(s_0 - 2)} 1 \tag{7.5}$$

$$= s_0 + \sum_{i=0}^{s_0 - 2} 2^i (s_1 - i) \tag{7.6}$$

$$= s_0 + \sum_{i=0}^{s_0 - 2} 2^i (s_0 - i - 1) \tag{7.7}$$

$$= 2^{s_0} - 1. \tag{7.8}$$

Adding the first node, which received the original query, one can see that the number of queries sent to different nodes matches exactly the number of different addresses that can be masked with the s_0 active bits of $f(m)$.

If the algorithm terminates early because the remaining bits inside the mask are managed locally, the query does not need to be forwarded any further and the number of forwards decreases.

After termination of the algorithm every node that can possibly contain a dataset queried for has sent its reply to the querying node. Thus, the query will be answered with all relevant datasets stored inside the distributed memory.

Locality Optimization

We introduce a very effective enhancement in order to reduce the latency generated by differences between CAN routing and IP routing for some common underlying network structures which is easy to implement. Every node announces its participation in the storage network using a layer-2 broadcast all over the local subnet or some comparable technique in non-ethernet environments. By receiving and replying to these broadcasts, every node can administrate a table of neighbors inside the same subnet that can be reached with a very low latency.

This additional neighbor table gives two advantages. Firstly, these neighbors can be preferred when routing through the DHT to lower the latency of the whole query. Secondly, these neighbors are distributed over the hash space and can be used as shortcuts to lower the number of query hops and thus, the latency as well.

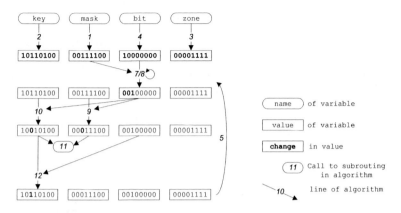

Figure 7.16: Forwarding algorithm for multiple data queries: The boxes represent the values of the corresponding variables in the algorithm as named above, the numbers from 1 to 12 represent the line of the pseudo code illustrated by the corresponding arrow and the highlighted bits are the ones that have been changed by the last algorithm step.

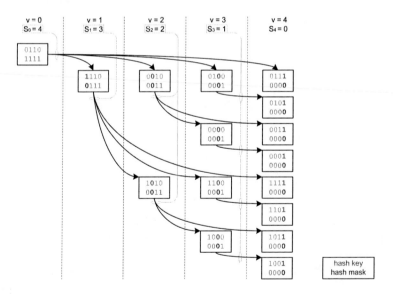

Figure 7.17: Transmissions due to the forwarding algorithm for multiple data queries: Every box represents a node that receives a query and forwards it after processing. Every arrow indicates one loop of the algorithm resulting in one forwarded query. The columns represent the different forwarding levels while one can see the number of forwards for a certain node in the rows.

Multiple Zones per Node

As stated in the introduction, a fill level of 50% and more leads to problems in data distribution over the CAN. To overcome this issue, we suggest to implement every CAN node to manage more than one CAN zone (m zones) by default. This way, the zones become smaller and more easy to move to different nodes. This results in more flexibility in data distribution.

A disadvantage of this solution is a higher number of total zones inside the CAN, which means that the maximum routing path length grows with a multiplier of $\sqrt[d]{m}$. The simulation will show whether this disadvantage can be compensated by the fact that any node now has m possibly well-distributed entry points into the CAN for its routing.

7.4.3 Implementation

The first step of our implementation strategy was the development of a simulator in order to verify the efficiency of our enhancements. Afterwards, we implemented the algorithm as an independent software solution with an easy-to-use network-based interface. Using this interface, our third step involved the development of a grid service to utilize our distributed associative memory in grid environments.

7.4.3.1 CAN Simulator for Java

Simulation of our enhancements, especially the verification of the efficiency of the locality enhancement, demanded the simulation of network environments to be as realistic as possible. Therefore, we decided to develop a very explicit simulator for network and storage simulation.

Our simulator follows a multi-layered architecture with three layers. The bottom layer is a very sophisticated ethernet simulator which emulates all kinds of network layouts. It reproduces the behavior of network-connections with given bandwidths and latencies. Furthermore, network equipment like routers, hubs and switches are simulated in much detail, including different routing and switching algorithms.

The middle layer is a local storage simulator to emulate different kinds of permanent storage for each node. The fundamentals are again bandwidth and, more important, latency. The simulator can distinguish between permanent storage and cache with different configurations.

The upper layer is represented by our CAN implementation itself. It utilizes the lower layers for communication and data storage. The behavior of our CAN implementation is highly configurable, especially when it comes to our three enhancements.

The simulator is developed using the JAVA language and benefits from its system independency. A multi threaded implementation featuring up to some thousand threads utilizes all available computing power.

Resulting from the very sophisticated reproduction of the networking and storage system the simulator can only emulate storage networks of up to few thousand nodes in an acceptable time frame. In return, the results are very close to reality.

7.4.3.2 The C-Implementation

The implementation of the CAN algorithm in the programming language C was intentionally done for two reasons:

1. simulation of larger networks (more than 20000 nodes) on our cluster computer and

2. application in real networks.

The application is splitted into two different parts, a server that stores data and a client that can query the data. Both applications are based on the Linux socket interface and are listening on a user-defined network socket for incoming CAN connections. To be able to join to a existing CAN network, as data node or for a query, the server/client needs to know the address and network port of any CAN server node. For data storage, a CAN server uses a Berkeley DB. So having more than one CAN data node on a single system is possible.

Queries for data in a CAN network are initialized by the CAN client. It sends a basic query to the specified CAN node. This node builds the CAN query, which is processed by the network and sends the data entries found back to the client.

With this implementation, we are able to instantiate a CAN network with 40000 nodes on the Linux cluster described in Section 7.3.2.1. The limiting units during this experiment are the count of processes and the available main memory and count of network sockets on the single cluster nodes.

7.4.3.3 Globus Grid Service

To use the associative memory network in grid environments, we implemented a CAN client for the Globus Toolkit [83]. Globus is an open source toolkit used for building grids. Among others it contains modules for communication, resource management, data management, and security. For the implementation the version 3.2 of the Globus Toolkit [84] is used and installed on the cluster described in Section 7.3.2.1 for testing. The CAN network runs independently of the Globus network.

Like the client implemented in the programming language C the Globus CAN client needs to know one initial CAN node. It is used to submit queries and receive answers of the network. Using this JAVA-based CAN interface it is possible to store and query data in a CAN distributed associative memory as a Globus Grid Service.

7.4.4 Verification of the Enhancements

Measurements took place in three simulated network topologies containing 45 to 500 nodes as a basis for the verification of the suggested methods. The first topology, Campus Sce-

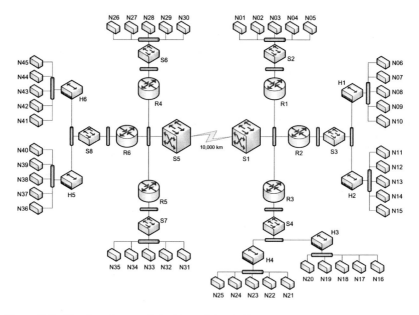

Figure 7.18: Topology layout of the Trans-Atlantic Scenario:
The central switches S1 and S5 are connected by a very long submarine cable introducing
a high latency into connections running from the networks on the left side to those on
the right side. On both sides there are 3 routers (Rx) attaching networks of 5 to 10
nodes (Nxx) with different numbers of switches (Sx) and hubs (Hx). The connections
between those routers and inside the attached networks provide different bandwidths but
introduce no noteworthy latencies.

nario, is a centralized one with only low-latency connections between 45 nodes. The
second one, Trans-Atlantic Scenario as pictured in Figure 7.18, also containing 45 nodes
uses two low-latency centers connected by a very long cable introducing high latencies.
Another simulation with 500 nodes connected in one local network was accomplished to
cross-check the results of the smaller simulations, especially for our multi zone enhancement.

Figure 7.19 illustrates the effect of our locality optimization. One can see that this
optimization has a negligible influence on Join operations while it speeds up Lookup as
well as Store operations. The speedup is even larger when one considers that the hard
drive of a node is simulated with an access latency of about 9 ms. That means at least 9
ms are required for accessing the hard disk to store the dataset inside or retrieve it from
the nodes' local storage system. Especially in the low-latency Campus Scenario, where
these 9 ms are more then 80% of the complete storing time, this consideration gives an

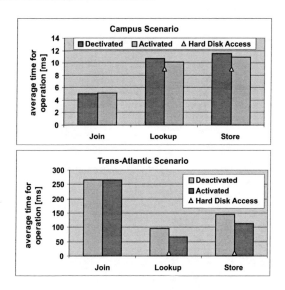

Figure 7.19: Influence of our locality-optimization on the average execution time for the given operations.

impression on the effective speedup of the locality optimization. The hard drive latency has no influence on Join operations because here, there is no dataset to be stored.

Figure 7.20 illustrates the effect of multiple zones per node on execution times. One can clearly see the immense negative influence on the average Join time of a node indicated by additional communication needs to synchronize zone information with a nodes new neighbors. Join operations into a data management system are by far more seldom than data based operations. And there seems to be almost no influence, neither positive nor negative, on Store and Lookup operations. Another simulation with 500 emulated nodes connected in one local subnet leads to a comparable result as shown in Figure 7.21.

7.4.5 Conclusions From the Simulation of our Enhancements

With our enhancements, we could greatly improve CAN as an algorithmic basis for a distributed storage system. Especially, the ability to answer to multiple data queries is of great importance. With our locality optimization, we could drastically reduce the latency and therefore, the time needed for Store and Lookup operations in the simulated network environments without a recognizable increase of time or network load for a Join operation.

By introducing the Query operation based on CAN, the algorithm provides a more efficient basis for distributed storage systems for grid environments. The ability to search for multiple keys by using a search mask can be of much use in scenarios where structured key information is available.

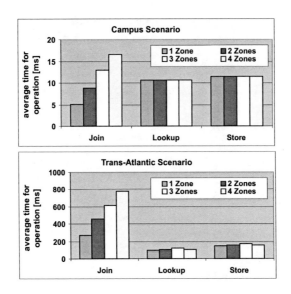

Figure 7.20: Influence of multiple zones per node on the average execution time for the given operations.

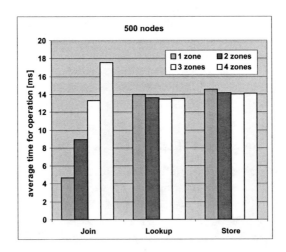

Figure 7.21: Average execution times for multiple zones per node in a simulation with 500 nodes.

The influence of multiple zones per node on Store and Lookup operations is very low while it greatly extends the time needed for a complete Join of a node into the CAN. This is acceptable in exchange for a more stable behavior, especially in surroundings with node joins and, more important, departures on distributed memories with high load. A dynamic implementation can be the next step in order to avoid the negative influence on node joins.

Part III

Conclusion and Future Research

Chapter 8

Conclusion and Future Research

8.1 Conclusions

We have presented a sound collection of benchmarks for distributed high-performance computers. The benchmarks measure all critical hardware, interconnect and software parts of a high performance computer: from the characteristics of main memory, disk access, inter-node communication, to scientific software architecture and software workload patterns. Based on the developed performance model, we are able to predict the performance of applications from the low-level characterization benchmarks.

In order to support an easy and efficient benchmarking cycle, we developed the IPACS software environment. This environment helps not only in the setup and execution of the benchmarks, but also with the analysis and comparison of the results. The proposed software architecture is robust and simple to be deployed in a wide variety of heterogeneous client environments. The data base design is elaborate enough to start with the benchmarking, but is also flexible in design to be easily adaptable to future requirements. The presentation of the benchmark results is designed to be most useful for the benchmark community. All results are immediately transferred to the web site via the repository server to make them available for comparison and analysis with other results.

The next step in the IPACS project is reaching a critical mass of data in the repository to obtain a meaningful base for investment decisions.

8.2 Future Work

To increase the number of benchmark results in the repository we will further develop adapters for HPC-batch systems and grid-environments to cover more HPC-systems. Future work will also include the handling of additional benchmark cases in coordination with the IPACS benchmark experts.

8.2.1   Performance Services for the Grid

A problem is that a grid scheduler must base its decisions on hand configured information, eventually together with online information of the availability of resources. At the moment, there is no conception of a finer grained scheduling also based on suitability of resources for certain applications or at performance parameters at all.

The idea is to provide a grid service for performance information based on the IPACS data warehouse and the IPACS framework for automatic execution of various benchmarks. This performance grid service can then be queried e.g. by a grid scheduler in order to get more information about the optimal matching between applications and resources. Also, applications can request computing resources based on fine-grained performance requirements.

In order to establish such a service, one would have to evaluate the Open Grid Services Architecture (OGSA) and Open Grid Services Infrastructure (OGSI) to understand all grid related service requirements. Then, a framework for this performance service, its query parameters and results must be developed. The performance analysis and evaluation would be based on the results from the (automatical) execution of the IPACS benchmarks on the requested grid computing resources. The IPACS data warehouse could then deliver information on performance anomalies between computing resources or on availability of certain performance levels.

Thus, the IPACS infrastructure could be exploited to offer an performance analysis and evaluation service for the HPC-Grid.

8.2.2   Development of a Performance Warehouse

Although the IPACS information retrieval component can offer many useful services, there is always more to request.

- IPACS does not provide the possibility to ask ad-hoc queries against the data warehouse, only predefined and developed queries are possible at the moment.

- There is no elaborate collaboration functionality, i.e. collaboration between users is limited to point-to-point email communication. One would also like to have a wiki or blog like functionality to directly comment on a single run of a benchmark or to make suggestions for improvements of benchmarks and their tuning, or even to object against certain results.

- It is not possible to directly connect the benchmark information to costs or to technical constraints (e.g. like power dissipation). Users would have to download benchmark data to their own Excel sheets and to connect this to inside cost and technical information. This would of course require a personalized access to the respective component.

- Using one's own performance prediction formulas in order to predict the performance of one's own applications. In IPACS we can only predict performance of applications from IPACS benchmark suite.

A technical use case for the performance warehouse could be the identification of computing systems based on complex relation ships like for example the ratio of the CPU performance to communication latency. An economical use case could be a optimized execution schedule for combined compute clusters and grid compute resources for a mix of applications. With the help of a personalized view to the performance warehouse one could add also site specific and computer specific cost information and use this to perform further business administration analysis.

The development of a performance warehouse will consist of several enhancements and new parts according to the business intelligence reference architecture (see section 5.1). The *data integration* component, which is already present in IPACS, would be enhanced by an integrator for e.g. grid service requests. The *data management* component can be taken with some minor modifications from the existing IPACS realization. The *information delivery* component must be enhanced by an ad-hoc query management part and a collaboration part. Predefined reports and graphics can be added for other questions of common interest. The component for *analytical applications* must be redeveloped from scratch. It can reuse parts from the existing performance prediction, but must have new subcomponents for historical analysis from the past to the future and a new subcomponent for business analysis and business assessment. The last subcomponent must have a personalized access to it. The *warehouse management* component must be extended by a security module to meet the personalization requirements of the collaboration and analytical application components.

The performance warehouse will allow easy access to information and insight from the stored performance data and will activate knowledge, which is incorporated within the IPACS data warehouse.

Part IV

Appendix

Appendix A

IPACS Publications

In this section the most important publications of the IPACS project are listed:

- 11/2005: 'Enhancements to CAN for the Applications as Distributed Data Storage System in Grids' 2nd International Workshop on Networks for Grid Applications, Boston, 2005

- 09/2005: Technical Article: 'The IPACS project at Glance' - IPACS Benchmark Suite, Performance Modeling and Prediction Methods, Benchmarking Environment This paper is an expanded and updated version of the article 'Integrated Performance Analysis of Computer Systems (IPACS) - Benchmarks for Distributed Computer Systems' published at PIK 3/05 (Praxis der Informationsverarbeitung und Kommunikation) in 2005.

- 09/2005: 'Workload-basierte Klassifikation von Benchmarks für lokale und verteilte I/O-Systeme' 3. GI/ITG-Workshop MMBnet 2005: Leistungs-, Zuverlässigkeits- und Verlässlichkeitsbewertung von Kommunikationsnetzen und verteilten Systemen, Hamburg, 2005

- 06/2005: 'Environment for I/O Performance Measurement of Distributed and Local Secondary Storage' International Workshop on Performance Evaluation of Networks, Parallel, Cluster and Grid Computing Systems, Oslo, 2005

- 02/2005: 'The PRIOMARKParallel I/O Benchmark' International Conference on Parallel and Distributed Computing and Networks, Innsbruck, 2005

- 06/2004: 'The Design of the IPACS Distributed Software Architecture' - Publication about the IPACS software architecture. Presentation at the 2nd Workshop on Distributed Objects Research, Experiences and Applications (DOREA 2), June 16-18, 2004, Las Vegas, USA in 3rd International Symposium on Information and Communication Technologies.

- 06/2004: 'A Mathematical Model for the Transitional Region between Cache Hierarchy Levels' International Workshop on Innovative Internet Computing Systems, Guadalajara, 2004

Appendix B

IPACS DTD

The listing B.1 shows the complete IPACS-DTD used by the IPACSrepository server
and benchmark client.

```xml
<?xml version="1.0" encoding="ISO-8859-1"?>
<!-- (C) IPACS, Matthias Merz                    -->
<!-- http://www.ipacs-benchmark.org/             -->
<!-- IPACS-Version 9, last change 23/11/2005 -->

<!ELEMENT ipacs (ipacs_header, ipacs_data?)>

<!ELEMENT ipacs_data (computer | computer_configuration |
    benchmark_request | benchmark_url_src | result_url |
    (benchmark_url, benchmark_url_src?)? | benchmark |
    known_cpus | available_benchmarks | known_sites | site |
    default_values | computer_id) >

<!ELEMENT ipacs_header ((error, exception?, stack_trace?) |
    (statement, parameter?, client_id?, client_version?))>

<!ELEMENT client_version (#PCDATA)>
<!ELEMENT statement (#PCDATA)>
<!ELEMENT parameter (#PCDATA)>
<!ELEMENT client_id (#PCDATA)>
<!ELEMENT computer_id (#PCDATA)>

<!ELEMENT computer (computer_name, computer_type,
    computer_architecture, computer_manufacturer)>
<!ELEMENT computer_architecture (#PCDATA)>
<!ELEMENT computer_manufacturer (#PCDATA)>

<!ELEMENT computer_name (#PCDATA)>
```

```
<!ELEMENT computer_type (#PCDATA)>
<!ELEMENT computer_configuration (hardware, software)>

<!ELEMENT benchmark_request (benchmark_name, benchmark_version,
    benchmark_type)>
<!ELEMENT benchmark_name (#PCDATA)>
<!ELEMENT benchmark_type (#PCDATA)>
<!ELEMENT benchmark_version (#PCDATA)>
<!ELEMENT benchmark_url (#PCDATA)>
<!ELEMENT benchmark_url_src (#PCDATA)>

<!ELEMENT result_url (#PCDATA)>

<!ELEMENT hardware (hardware_class?, (inter_connect+)?, node? )>
<!ELEMENT hardware_class (#PCDATA)>
<!ELEMENT inter_connect (inter_connect_name)>
<!ELEMENT inter_connect_name (#PCDATA)>

<!ELEMENT node (number_of_nodes?, cpu?, cache?, ram?)>
<!ELEMENT number_of_nodes (#PCDATA)>

<!ELEMENT known_cpus (cpu?)+>

<!ELEMENT cpu (cpu_name?, cpu_vendor?, cpu_speed?,
    cpu_fp_operations?, number_of_cpus_per_node?)>
<!ELEMENT cpu_name (#PCDATA)>
<!ELEMENT cpu_vendor (#PCDATA)>
<!ELEMENT cpu_speed (#PCDATA)>
<!ELEMENT cpu_fp_operations (#PCDATA)>
<!ELEMENT number_of_cpus_per_node (#PCDATA)>
<!ELEMENT cache (cache_size)>
<!ELEMENT cache_size (#PCDATA)>
<!ELEMENT ram (ram_name?, ram_capacity?)>
<!ELEMENT ram_name (#PCDATA)>
<!ELEMENT ram_capacity (#PCDATA)>

<!ELEMENT software (cluster_software?, compiler?, operating_system?
    tool?)>
<!ELEMENT cluster_software (mpi_library?, mpi_device?, mpi_path?,
    mpicc?, mpicxx?)>
<!ELEMENT mpi_library (#PCDATA)>
```

```
<!ELEMENT mpi_device (#PCDATA)>
<!ELEMENT mpi_path (#PCDATA)>
<!ELEMENT mpicc (#PCDATA)>
<!ELEMENT mpicxx (#PCDATA)>


<!ELEMENT compiler (compiler_c?, compiler_f77?, compiler_f90?)>
<!ELEMENT compiler_c (#PCDATA)>
<!ELEMENT compiler_f77 (#PCDATA)>
<!ELEMENT compiler_f90 (#PCDATA)>
<!ELEMENT operating_system (os_name?, os_version?)>
<!ELEMENT os_name (#PCDATA)>

<!ELEMENT os_version (#PCDATA)>
<!ELEMENT tool (tool_name)>
<!ELEMENT tool_name (#PCDATA)>


<!ELEMENT available_benchmarks (benchmark+)>

<!-- benchmark is used by available_benchmarks and sbumit_result-->
<!ELEMENT benchmark (name, version?, sub_benchmark?, website?,
    directlyExecutable?)>
<!ELEMENT name (#PCDATA)>
<!ELEMENT version (#PCDATA)>
<!ELEMENT directlyExecutable (#PCDATA)>
<!ELEMENT website (#PCDATA)>
<!ELEMENT sub_benchmark (name, processors, characteristic_number+,
    detailed_output)>
<!ELEMENT processors (#PCDATA)>
<!ELEMENT characteristic_number (name, value)>
<!ELEMENT value (#PCDATA)>
<!ELEMENT detailed_output (#PCDATA | file )*>
<!ELEMENT file (#PCDATA)>


<!ELEMENT known_sites (site+)>
<!ELEMENT site (site_name, site_country, site_area, site_address,
    site_city, site_contact_person?, site_contact_phone?,
    site_contact_mail?, site_web_url?)>
<!ELEMENT site_id (#PCDATA)>
<!ELEMENT site_name (#PCDATA)>
<!ELEMENT site_country (#PCDATA)>
<!ELEMENT site_area (#PCDATA)>
```

```
<!ELEMENT site_address (#PCDATA)>
<!ELEMENT site_city (#PCDATA)>
<!ELEMENT site_contact_person (#PCDATA)>
<!ELEMENT site_contact_phone (#PCDATA)>
<!ELEMENT site_contact_mail (#PCDATA)>
<!ELEMENT site_web_url (#PCDATA)>

<!ELEMENT default_values (item+)>
<!ELEMENT item (#PCDATA)>

<!ELEMENT error (#PCDATA)>
<!ELEMENT exception (#PCDATA)>
<!ELEMENT line (#PCDATA)>
<!ELEMENT stack_trace (line+)>

<!ATTLIST site site_id CDATA #IMPLIED>
<!ATTLIST file name CDATA #REQUIRED type CDATA #REQUIRED>
```

Listing B.1: IPACS-DTD

Appendix C

IPACS Entity Relationship Model

This section outlines the complete entity relationship diagram of the IPACS repository server on the next two pages. The corresponding data model of the database could be found in appendix D.

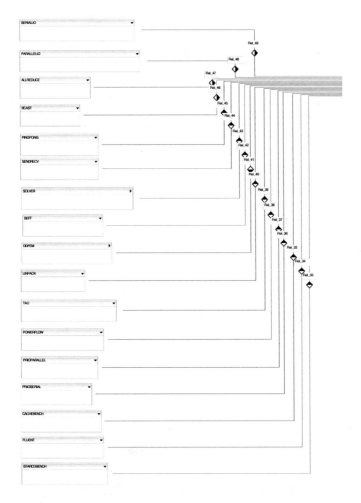

Figure C.1: Complete Entity Relationship Diagram (Part I).

XXI

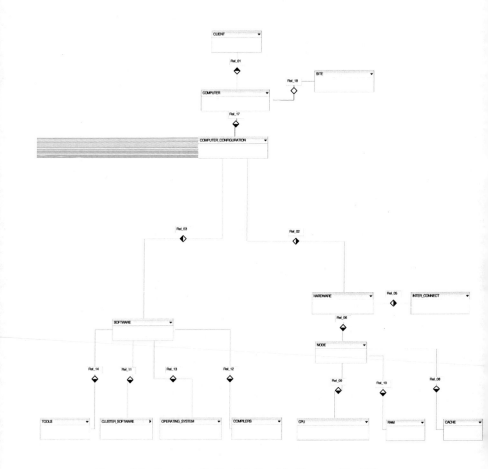

Figure C.2: Complete Entity Relationship Diagram (Part II).

Appendix D

IPACS Database Model

The tables in this section reflect the data model of the repository server's database. The corresponding entity relationship diagram could be found in appendix C.

Table D.1: Structure of ALLREDUCE

Feld	Typ	Null
ALLREDUCE_ID	bigint(20)	Nein
ALLREDUCE_DATE	datetime	Nein
ALLREDUCE_CONFIGURATION	bigint(20)	Ja
ALLREDUCE_PROCESSORS	int(11)	Ja
ALLREDUCE_LATENCY	double	Ja
ALLREDUCE_TIME_AT_4MB	double	Ja
ALLREDUCE_ASCII	text	Ja

Table D.2: Structure of BCAST

Feld	Typ	Null
BCAST_ID	bigint(20)	Nein
BCAST_DATE	datetime	Nein
BCAST_CONFIGURATION	bigint(20)	Ja
BCAST_PROCESSORS	int(11)	Ja
BCAST_LATENCY	double	Ja
BCAST_TIME_AT_4MB	double	Ja
BCAST_ASCII	text	Ja

Table D.3: Structure of B_{eff}

Feld	Typ	Null
BEFF_ID	bigint(20)	Nein

Table D.3: Structure of B$_{eff}$

Feld	Typ	Null
BEFF_DATE	datetime	Nein
BEFF_CONFIGURATION	bigint(20)	Ja
BEFF_PROCESSORS	int(11)	Ja
BEFF_ACCUMULATED_BANDWIDTH	double	Ja
BEFF_ASCII	text	Ja

Table D.4: Structure of CACHE

Feld	Typ	Null
CACHE_ID	bigint(20)	Nein
CACHE_SIZE	varchar(30)	Ja
NODE_ID	bigint(20)	Ja

Table D.5: Structure of CACHEBENCH

Feld	Typ	Null
CACHEBENCH_ID	bigint(20)	Nein
CACHEBENCH_DATE	datetime	Nein
CACHEBENCH_CONFIGURATION	bigint(20)	Ja
CACHEBENCH_PROCESSORS	int(11)	Ja
CACHEBENCH_CACHEBENCHREAD	double	Ja
CACHEBENCH_CACHEBENCHWRITE	double	Ja
CACHEBENCH_CACHEBENCHRMW	double	Ja
CACHEBENCH_ASCII	text	Ja
CACHEBENCH_JPG	longblob	Ja
CACHEBENCH_PS	longblob	Ja

Table D.6: Structure of CLIENT

Feld	Typ	Null
CLIENT_ID	int(11)	Nein
IP_ADDRESS	varchar(30)	Ja
LAST_STATEMENT	varchar(255)	Ja
COMPUTER_ID	int(11)	Ja
CLIENT_DATE	datetime	Nein

Table D.7: Structure of CLUSTER_SOFTWARE

Feld	Typ	Null
CLUSTER_ID	bigint(20)	Nein
MPI_LIBRARY	varchar(30)	Ja
MPI_DEVICE	varchar(30)	Ja
MPI_PATH	varchar(100)	Ja
MPICC	varchar(100)	Ja
MPICXX	varchar(100)	Ja
SOFTWARE_ID	bigint(20)	Ja

Table D.8: Structure of COMPILERS

Feld	Typ	Null
COMPILER_ID	bigint(20)	Nein
COMPILER_C	varchar(100)	Ja
COMPILER_F77	varchar(100)	Ja
COMPILER_F90	varchar(100)	Ja
SOFTWARE_ID	bigint(20)	Ja

Table D.9: Structure of COMPUTER

Feld	Typ	Null
COMPUTER_ID	int(11)	Nein
COMPUTER_SITE	int(11)	Ja
COMPUTER_NAME	varchar(255)	Nein
COMPUTER_TYPE	varchar(255)	Ja
COMPUTER_ARCHITECTURE	varchar(255)	Ja
COMPUTER_MANUFACTURER	varchar(255)	Ja
COMPUTER_INSERT_DATE	date	Nein

Table D.10: Structure of COMPUTER_CONFIGURATION

Feld	Typ	Null
CONFIGURATION_ID	bigint(20)	Nein
CONFIGURATION_DATE	datetime	Ja
COMPUTER	int(11)	Ja

Table D.11: Structure of CPU

Feld	Typ	Null
CPU_ID	bigint(20)	Nein
CPU_NAME	varchar(30)	Ja
CPU_VENDOR	varchar(30)	Ja
CPU_SPEED	float	Ja
CPU_FP_OPERATIONS	int(3)	Ja
NUMBER_OF_CPUS_PER_NODE	int(5)	Ja
NODE_ID	bigint(20)	Ja

Table D.12: Structure of DDFEM

Feld	Typ	Null
DDFEM_ID	bigint(20)	Nein
DDFEM_DATE	datetime	Nein
DDFEM_CONFIGURATION	bigint(20)	Ja
DDFEM_PROCESSORS	int(11)	Ja
DDFEM_TOTAL_FLOP	double	Ja
DDFEM_TOTL_NUM_OF_ACTIVE_NODES	double	Ja
DDFEM_MPI_MESSAGES	double	Ja
DDFEM_ASCII	text	Ja

Table D.13: Structure of DEFAULTVALUES

Feld	Typ	Null
HARDWARE_CLASS	varchar(30)	Ja
COMPUTER_ARCHITECTURE	varchar(30)	Ja
COMPUTER_MANUFACTURER	varchar(255)	Ja

Table D.14: Structure of FLUENT

Feld	Typ	Null
FLUENT_ID	bigint(20)	Nein
FLUENT_DATE	datetime	Nein
FLUENT_CONFIGURATION	bigint(20)	Ja
FLUENT_PROCESSORS	int(11)	Ja
FLUENT_TOTAL_WALL_CLOCK_TIME	double	Ja
FLUENT_TOTAL_CPU_TIME	double	Ja
FLUENT_ITERATION_TRANSFER	double	Ja

Table D.14: Structure of FLUENT

Feld	Typ	Null
FLUENT_ASCII	text	Ja

Table D.15: Structure of HARDWARE

Feld	Typ	Null
HARDWARE_ID	bigint(20)	Nein
HARDWARE_CLASS	varchar(30)	Ja
CONFIGURATION_ID	bigint(20)	Ja

Table D.16: Structure of INTER_CONNECT

Feld	Typ	Null
INTER_CONNECT_ID	bigint(20)	Nein
INTER_CONNECT_NAME	varchar(30)	Ja
HARDWARE_ID	bigint(20)	Ja

Table D.17: Structure of KNOWN_CPUS

Feld	Typ	Null
CPU_ID	bigint(20)	Nein
CPU_NAME	varchar(30)	Ja
CPU_VENDOR	varchar(30)	Ja
CPU_FP_OPERATIONS	int(3)	Ja
MATCH_STRING	varchar(255)	Nein

Table D.18: Structure of LINPACK

Feld	Typ	Null
LINPACK_ID	bigint(20)	Nein
LINPACK_DATE	datetime	Nein
LINPACK_CONFIGURATION	bigint(20)	Ja
LINPACK_PROCESSORS	int(11)	Ja
LINPACK_RMAX	double	Ja
LINPACK_NMAX	double	Ja
LINPACK_NBMAX	double	Ja
LINPACK_RHALF	double	Ja
LINPACK_NHALF	double	Ja

Table D.18: Structure of LINPACK

Feld	Typ	Null
LINPACK_NBHALF	double	Ja
LINPACK_ASCII	text	Ja

Table D.19: Structure of NODE

Feld	Typ	Null
NODE_ID	bigint(20)	Nein
NUMBER_OF_NODES	int(6)	Ja
HARDWARE_ID	bigint(20)	Ja

Table D.20: Structure of OPERATING_SYSTEM

Feld	Typ	Null
OS_ID	bigint(20)	Nein
SOFTWARE_OS	varchar(50)	Ja
SOFTWARE_OS_VERSION	varchar(50)	Ja
SOFTWARE_ID	bigint(20)	Ja

Table D.21: Structure of PARALLELIO

Feld	Typ	Null
PARALLELIO_ID	bigint(20)	Nein
PARALLELIO_DATE	datetime	Nein
PARALLELIO_CONFIGURATION	bigint(20)	Ja
PARALLELIO_PROCESSORS	int(11)	Ja
PARALLELIO_FLUID_GRID_POINT_CALCULATION_RATE	double	Ja
PARALLELIO_FLOATING_POINT_OPERATION_RATE	double	Ja
PARALLELIO_TOTAL_IO_TIME_WRITE	double	Ja
PARALLELIO_TOTAL_IO_RATE_WRITE	double	Ja
PARALLELIO_TOTAL_IO_TIME_READ	double	Ja
PARALLELIO_TOTAL_IO_RATE_READ	double	Ja
PARALLELIO_ASCII	text	Ja

Table D.22: Structure of PINGPONG

Feld	Typ	Null
PINGPONG_ID	bigint(20)	Nein

Table D.22: Structure of PINGPONG

Feld	Typ	Null
PINGPONG_DATE	datetime	Nein
PINGPONG_CONFIGURATION	bigint(20)	Ja
PINGPONG_PROCESSORS	int(11)	Ja
PINGPONG_LATENCY	double	Ja
PINGPONG_MAX_BANDWIDTH	double	Ja
PINGPONG_BANDWIDTH_AT_4MB	double	Ja
PINGPONG_ASCII	text	Ja

Table D.23: Structure of POWERFLOW

Feld	Typ	Null
POWERFLOW_ID	bigint(20)	Nein
POWERFLOW_DATE	datetime	Nein
POWERFLOW_CONFIGURATION	bigint(20)	Ja
POWERFLOW_PROCESSORS	int(11)	Ja
POWERFLOW_CALCULATION_RATIO	double	Ja
POWERFLOW_SIMULATION_TIME	double	Ja
POWERFLOW_ASCII	text	Ja

Table D.24: Structure of PRIOPARALLEL

Feld	Typ	Null
PRIOPARALLEL_ID	bigint(20)	Nein
PRIOPARALLEL_DATE	datetime	Nein
PRIOPARALLEL_CONFIGURATION	bigint(20)	Ja
PRIOPARALLEL_PROCESSORS	int(11)	Ja
PRIOPARALLEL_COMMONFILE	double	Ja
PRIOPARALLEL_SINGLEFILE	double	Ja
PRIOPARALLEL_STRIDEDFILE	double	Ja
PRIOPARALLEL_COLLECTEDDISK	double	Ja
PRIOPARALLEL_ASCII	text	Ja
PRIOPARALLEL_JPG1	longblob	Ja
PRIOPARALLEL_PS1	longblob	Ja
PRIOPARALLEL_JPG2	longblob	Ja
PRIOPARALLEL_PS2	longblob	Ja

Table D.25: Structure of PRIOSERIAL

Feld	Typ	Null
PRIOSERIAL_ID	bigint(20)	Nein
PRIOSERIAL_DATE	datetime	Nein
PRIOSERIAL_CONFIGURATION	bigint(20)	Ja
PRIOSERIAL_PROCESSORS	int(11)	Ja
PRIOSERIAL_SINGLEFILE	double	Ja
PRIOSERIAL_COLLECTEDDISK	double	Ja
PRIOSERIAL_ASCII	text	Ja
PRIOSERIAL_JPG	longblob	Ja
PRIOSERIAL_PS	longblob	Ja

Table D.26: Structure of RAM

Feld	Typ	Null
RAM_ID	bigint(20)	Nein
RAM_NAME	varchar(30)	Ja
CAPACITY	varchar(30)	Ja
NODE_ID	bigint(20)	Ja

Table D.27: Structure of SENDRECV

Feld	Typ	Null
SENDRECV_ID	bigint(20)	Nein
SENDRECV_DATE	datetime	Nein
SENDRECV_CONFIGURATION	bigint(20)	Ja
SENDRECV_PROCESSORS	int(11)	Ja
SENDRECV_LATENCY	double	Ja
SENDRECV_BANDWIDTH_AT_4MB	double	Ja
SENDRECV_MAX_BANDWIDTH	double	Ja
SENDRECV_ASCII	text	Ja

Table D.28: Structure of SERIALIO

Feld	Typ	Null
SERIALIO_ID	bigint(20)	Nein
SERIALIO_DATE	datetime	Nein
SERIALIO_CONFIGURATION	bigint(20)	Ja
SERIALIO_PROCESSORS	int(11)	Ja

Table D.28: Structure of SERIALIO

Feld	Typ	Null
SERIALIO_FLUID_GRID_POINT_CALCULATION_RATE	double	Ja
SERIALIO_FLOATING_POINT_OPERATION_RATE	double	Ja
SERIALIO_TOTAL_IO_TIME_WRITE	double	Ja
SERIALIO_TOTAL_IO_RATE_WRITE	double	Ja
SERIALIO_TOTAL_IO_TIME_READ	double	Ja
SERIALIO_TOTAL_IO_RATE_READ	double	Ja
SERIALIO_ASCII	text	Ja

Table D.29: Structure of SITE

Feld	Typ	Null
SITE_ID	int(11)	Nein
SITE_NAME	varchar(100)	Ja
SITE_COUNTRY	varchar(100)	Ja
SITE_AREA	varchar(100)	Ja
SITE_ADDRESS	varchar(100)	Ja
SITE_CITY	varchar(100)	Ja
SITE_CONTACT_PERSON	varchar(100)	Ja
SITE_CONTACT_PHONE	varchar(100)	Ja
SITE_CONTACT_MAIL	varchar(100)	Ja
SITE_WEB_URL	varchar(150)	Ja

Table D.30: Structure of SOFTWARE

Feld	Typ	Null
SOFTWARE_ID	bigint(20)	Nein
CONFIGURATION_ID	bigint(20)	Ja

Table D.31: Structure of SOLVER

Feld	Typ	Null
SOLVER_ID	bigint(20)	Nein
SOLVER_DATE	datetime	Nein
SOLVER_CONFIGURATION	bigint(20)	Ja
SOLVER_PROCESSORS	int(11)	Ja
SOLVER_FLUID_GRID_POINT_CALCULATION_RATE	double	Ja
SOLVER_FLOATING_POINT_OPERATION_RATE	double	Ja

Table D.31: Structure of SOLVER

Feld	Typ	Null
SOLVER_ASCII	text	Ja

Table D.32: Structure of STARCDBENCH

Feld	Typ	Null
STARCDBENCH_ID	bigint(20)	Nein
STARCDBENCH_DATE	datetime	Nein
STARCDBENCH_CONFIGURATION	bigint(20)	Ja
STARCDBENCH_PROCESSORS	int(11)	Ja
STARCDBENCH_CALCULATION_RATIO	double	Ja
STARCDBENCH_ELAPSED_TIME	double	Ja
STARCDBENCH_ASCII	text	Ja

Table D.33: Structure of TAU

Feld	Typ	Null
TAU_ID	bigint(20)	Nein
TAU_DATE	datetime	Nein
TAU_CONFIGURATION	bigint(20)	Ja
TAU_PROCESSORS	int(11)	Ja
TAU_FLOATING_POINT_OPERATION_RATE	double	Ja
TAU_GRID_POINTS	int(11)	Ja
TAU_COMMUNICATION_RATIO	double	Ja
TAU_ASCII	text	Ja

Table D.34: Structure of TOOLS

Feld	Typ	Null
TOOL_ID	bigint(20)	Nein
TOOL_NAME	varchar(30)	Ja
SOFTWARE_ID	bigint(20)	Ja

Appendix E

Repository Server Error Messages

Table E.1 on the next page show the complete error code list for the repository server. The List is separated into the different categories communication, database, XML, logical, benchmark client and other errors.

Error-Number	Description
Communication-Errors	
1000	Method `doGet` unsupported.
1010	General IPACS server error.
1020	General IPACS server problem with the XML DOM-Parser.
Database-Errors	
2010	No connection to database.
2020	JDBC-Error by getting Client-ID.
2030	General JDBC-Error.
2040	Column `<column>` not found.
XML-Errors	
3000	Incoming XML message could not be validated against the IPACS-DTD.
3010	`<statement>`-tag is empty.
3020	Statement `<statement>` unknown.
3030	Client-ID is empty.
3040	Field "Computer_name" is empty.
3050	Computer-ID is not an integer.
3080	Filed "Benchmark_name" is empty.
3081	Field "Benchmark_type" is empty.
3082	Filed "Benchmark_version" is empty.
3090	Filed "Benchmark_type" must be source or binary.
3120	The given Computer-Configuration ID is not an integer.
Logical Errors	
4000	Site-Information must be entered before submitting a benchmark result.
4010	Can't store a computer configuration without an entry in table computer.
4020	Client_id `<client_id>` wrong.
4030	No entry in Table computer for Client-ID `<client_id>`.
4040	No binary and source Benchmark available.
4050	Client_id `<client_id>` unknown.
4060	Changing IP-address failed.
4070	Security-Error: Incoming and stored IP-Address are different.
Benchmark Client Errors	
8000	Version of IPACS-client is to old.
Other Errors	
9999	Test-message.

Table E.1: Repository Server: Error Codes

Bibliography

[1] TOP500 Supercomputer Sites. http://www.top500.org/, 2005.

[2] Netlib. High performance Linpack (HPL) at netlib. http://www.netlib.org/benchmark/hpl/, 2005.

[3] D. H. Bailey, E. Barszcz, J. T. Barton, D. S. Browning, R. L. Carter, D. Dagum, R. A. Fatoohi, P. O. Frederickson, T. A. Lasinski, R. S. Schreiber, H. D. Simon, V. Venkatakrishnan, and S. K. Weeratunga. The NAS Parallel Benchmarks. *The International Journal of Supercomputer Applications*, 5(3):63–73, Fall 1991.

[4] NAS Parallel Benchmark (NPB). http://www.nas.nasa.gov/Software/NPB/, 2005.

[5] Standard Performance Evaluation Corporation (SPEC). http://www.specbench.org/, 2005.

[6] Transaction Processing Council (TPC). http://www.tpc.org/, 2004.

[7] IPACS. Integrated Performance Analysis of Computer Systems. http://www.ipacs-benchmark.org/, 2005.

[8] Franz-Josef Pfreundt and Matthias Merz. The IPACS project - a New Benchmarking Environment. In *International Supercomputer Conference ISC2004, June 23-25, Heidelberg, Germany*. MATEO, 2004.

[9] Innovative Computing Laboratory. Repository in a Box (RIB). http://icl.cs.utk.edu/rib/, 2005.

[10] Netlib. Performance Database Server. http://performance.netlib.org/performance/html/PDStop.html, 2005.

[11] Performance Evaluation Research Center (PERC). http://perc.nersc.gov/, 2005.

[12] HPC Challenge. HPC Challenge. http://icl.cs.utk.edu/hpcc/, 2005.

[13] San Diego Supercomputer Center at UCSD. Performance Modeling and Characterization (PaMaC). http://www.sdsc.edu/PMaC/Benchmark/, 2004.

[14] International Data Corporation (IDC). HPC User Forum.
     http://www.hpcuserforum.com/, 2005.

[15] Aad van der Steen. How informative is the IDC balanced rating HPC benchmark?
     http://www.hoise.com/primeur/02/articles/weekly/AE-PR-03-02-60.html, 2002.

[16] William Gropp, Steven Huss-Lederman, Andrew Lumsdaine, Ewing Lusk, Bill
     Nitzberg, William Saphir, and Marc Snir. *MPI — The Complete Reference: Volume
     2, the MPI-2 Extensions*. MIT Press, 1998.

[17] Bonnie Benchmark. http://www.textuality.com/bonnie, 2005.

[18] IOzone Filesystem Benchmark. http://www.iozone.org/, 2005.

[19] R. Rabenseifner and A.E. Koniges. The Effective I/O Bandwidth Benchmark
     (b_eff_io). In *Proceedings of the Message Passing Interface Developer's Conference*,
     2000.

[20] Michael Krietemeyer, Daniel Versick, and Djamshid Tavangarian. The PRIOmark
     – Parallel I/O Benchmark. In *Proceedings of the IASTED International Conference
     on Parallel and Distributed Computing and Networks*, pages 595 – 600, 2005.

[21] B. Pawlowski, C. Juszczak, P. Staubach, C. Smith, D. Lebel, and D. Hitz. NFS
     Version 3: Design and Implementation. In *Proceedings of Summer 1994 USENIX
     Conference*, pages 137 – 152, 1994.

[22] GFS. Red Hat Cluster Project Page. http://sources.redhat.com/cluster, 2005.

[23] GFS. Red Hat GFS 6.0 Administrator's Guide.
     http://www.redhat.com/docs/manuals/csgfs/admin-guide, 2005.

[24] Lustre. Lustre: A Scalable, High-Performance File System.
     http://www.lustre.org/docs/whitepaper.pdf, 2005.

[25] P. H. Carns, W. B. Ligon III, R. B. Ross, and R. Thakur. PVFS: A Parallel File
     System for Linux Clusters. In *Proceedings of the 4th Annual Linux Showcase and
     Conference*, pages 317 – 327, 2000.

[26] Philip J. Mucci, Kevin London, and John Thurman. The CacheBench Report.
     http://icl.cs.utk.edu/projects/llcbench/cachebench.pdf, 1998.

[27] Pallas MPI Benchmarks (PMB).
     http://www.pallas.com/pages/pmb.htm, 2003.

[28] Philip J. Mucci. LLCbench - Low-Level Characterization Benchmarks.
     http://icl.cs.utk.edu/projects/llcbench, 2005.

[29] ITWM. Institut für Techno- und Wirtschaftsmathematik.
      http://www.itwm.fhg.de, 2005.

[30] D-Grid Initiative. http://www.d-grid.de/.

[31] EGEE. http://egee-intranet.web.cern.ch/egee-intranet/gateway.html.

[32] TeraGrid. http://www.teragrid.org/.

[33] H. Casanova G. Chun, H. Dail and A. Snavely. Benchmark probes for grid assessment.
      In *18th International Parallel and Distributed Processing Symposium (IPDPS'04)*,
      2004.

[34] Intel Corporation. Intel Xeon Processor.
      http://www.intel.com/products/processor/xeon/, 2005.

[35] C. Guiang, A. Purkayastha, Milfeld K., and J. Boisseau. Memory performance of
      dual-processor nodes: comparison of Intel Xeon and AMD Opteron memory sub-
      system architectures. In *Proceedings of the ClusterWorld Conference and Expo*, San
      Jose, CA, 2003.

[36] Fluent Benchmarks. http://www.fluent.com/software/fluent/fl5bench/intro.htm,
      2005.

[37] B. Humm and F. Wietek. Architektur von Data Warehouses. *Informatik Spektrum*,
      02:3–14, 2005.

[38] Heinz Kredel and Matthias Merz. The Design of the IPACS Distributed Software
      Architecture. In *3rd International Symposium on Information and Communication
      Technologies, Second Workshop on Distributed Objects Research, Experiences and
      Applications (DOREA)*, A Volume in the ACM international conference proceedings
      series, pages 14–19, Las Vegas, 2004. Computer Science Press.

[39] Sun Microsystems. Java 2 Platform Enterprise Edition 1.4.
      java.sun.com/j2ee/, 2003.

[40] Sun Microsystems. Enterprise JavaBeans Specification 2.1.
      java.sun.com/products/ejb/, 2003.

[41] Java Community Process. JSR-154, Servlet 2.4 Specification.
      http://www.jcp.org/en/jsr/detail?id=154, 2003.

[42] Apache Software Foundation. The Jakarta project - Tomcat.
      http://jakarta.apache.org/tomcat/index.html, 2004.

[43] Malcolm Atkinson, François Bancilhon, D. DeWitt, Klaus Dittrich, David Maier,
      and Stanley Zdonik. The object-oriented database system manifesto. In *Proceedings*

of the First International Conference on Deductive and Object-Oriented Databases (DOOD'89), pages 223–240, Kyoto, Japan, 1989. North-Holland/Elsevier Science Publishers.

[44] Alexandra Schäfer. Der "impedance mismatch": Im spannungsfeld zwischen objektorientiertem und relationalem ansatz. *Objektspektrum*, 3:S. 33–36, 2003.

[45] Java Community Process. Java data objects specification 1.0.1 (JDO). http://www.jcp.org/en/jsr/detail?id=12, 2003.

[46] Axel Korthaus and Matthias Merz. A Critical Analysis of JDO in the Context of J2EE. In Al-Ani Ban, H. R. Arabnia, and Mun Youngsong, editors, *Proceedings of the 2003 International Conference on Software Engineering Research and Practice (SERP '03)*, volume I, pages 34–40. CSREA Press, 2003.

[47] Matthias Merz. Using the Dynamic Proxy Approach to Introduce Role-Based Security to Java Data Objects. Eighteenth International Conference on Software Engineering and Knowledge Engineering (SEKE'06), San Francisco, USA, July, 2006.

[48] Sun Microsystems, Inc. *Java Beans*. http://www.javasoft.com/beans.

[49] ECMA standards organization. ECMA-262, ECMAScript : A general purpose, cross-platform programming language. http://www.ecma-international.org/publications/standards/, 1997.

[50] Sun Microsystems, Inc. Java Applets. http://java.sun.com/applets/.

[51] Java Community Process. JSR-152, JavaServer Pages 2.0 Specification. http://java.sun.com/products/jsp/, 2003.

[52] Sun Microsystems, Inc. Java Web Start Technology. http://java.sun.com/products/javawebstart/.

[53] Erich Gamma, Richard Helm, Ralph Johnson, and John Vlissides. *Design Patterns: Elements of Reusable Object-Oriented Software*. Addison Wesley, Massachusetts, 1994.

[54] Interdisciplinary Center for Scientific Computing. HELICS: HEidelberg LInux Cluster System. http://helics.uni-hd.de.

[55] JCraft. JSch - Java Secure Channel. http://www.jcraft.com/jsch/.

[56] T. Gerhold, O. Friedrich, J. Evans, and M. Galle. Calculation of Complex Three-Dimensional Configurations Employing the DLR-TAU-Code. *AIAA*, 97-0167, 1997.

[57] John L. Hennessy and David A. Patterson. *Computer architecture (2nd ed.): a quantitative approach.* Morgan Kaufmann Publishers Inc., San Francisco, CA, USA, 1996.

[58] Bill O. Gallmeister. *POSIX.4: programming for the real world.* O'Reilly & Associates, Inc., Sebastopol, CA, USA, 1995.

[59] Michael J. Flynn. Very High Speed Computing Systems. *Proceedings of the IEEE*, 54:1901–1909, 1966.

[60] Garth A. Gibson and Rodney van Meter. Network Attached Storage Architecture. *Communications of the ACM*, 43(11):37–45, 2000.

[61] Paul Leach and Dan Perry. CIFS: A Common Internet File System. http://www.microsoft.com/mind/1196/cifs.asp, 1996.

[62] Peter M. Chen, Edward K. Lee, Garth A. Gibson, Randy H. Katz, and David A. Patterson. RAID: High-Performance, Reliable Secondary Storage. *ACM Computing Surveys*, 26(2):145–185, 1994.

[63] R. K. Khattar, M. S. Murphy, G. J. Tarella, and K. E. Nystrom. Introduction to Storage Area Network. Redbooks Publications (IBM), 1999.

[64] IOR_MPIIO. The IOR README File. Lawrence Livermore National Laboratory, http://www.llnl.gov/asci/purple/benchmarks/limited/ior/ior.mpiio.readme.html, 2001.

[65] Peter M. Chen and David A. Patterson. A New Approach to I/O Performance Evaluation – Self-Scaling I/O Benchmarks, Predicted I/O Performance. *ACM Transactions on Computer Systems*, 12(4):308–339, 1994.

[66] Parkson Wong and Rob F. Van der Wijngaart. NAS Parallel Benchmarks I/O Version 2.4. Technical Report Technical Report NAS-03-002, NASA Advanced Supercomputing (NAS) Division, NASA Ames Research Center, 2003.

[67] Barry L. Wolman and Thomas M. Olson. IOBENCH: A System Independent IO Benchmark. *Computer Architecture News*, 1989.

[68] Philip M. Papadopoulos, Mason J. Katz, and Greg Bruno. NPACI Rocks Clusters: Tools for Easily Deploying and Maintaining Manageable High-Performance Linux Clusters. In *Proceedings of the 8th European PVM/MPI Users' Group Meeting on Recent Advances in Parallel Virtual Machine and Message Passing Interface*, pages 10–11, London, UK, 2001. Springer-Verlag.

[69] William Gropp, Ewing Lusk, Nathan Doss, and Anthony Skjellum. A High-Performance, Portable Implementation of the MPI Message Passing Interface Standard. *Parallel Computing*, 22(6):789–828, 1996.

[70] Rajeev Thakur, William Gropp, and Ewing Lusk. On Implementing MPI-IO Portably and With High Performance. In *IOPADS '99: Proceedings of the Sixth Workshop on I/O in Parallel and Distributed Systems*, pages 23–32, New York, NY, USA, 1999. ACM Press.

[71] Stephen Tweedie. Ext3, Journaling Filesystem. Ottawa Linux Symposium 2000. http://olstrans.sourceforge.net/release/OLS2000-ext3/OLS2000-ext3.html.

[72] F. Wang, Q. Xin, B. Hong, S. Brandt, E. Miller, D. Long, and T. McLarty. File System Workload Analysis for Large Scale Scientific Computing Applications. In *Proceedings of the 21st IEEE / 12th NASA Goddard Conference on Mass Storage Systems and Technologies*, 2004.

[73] Lustre. The Lustre Storage Architecture. http://www.lustre.org/docs/lustre.pdf.

[74] I. Foster. The Grid: A New Infrastructure for the 21st Century Science. *Physics Today*, Febuary 2002.

[75] P. LGuy, E. Kunszt, H. Laure, and K. Stockinger. Replica Management in Data Grids. In *Proceedings of Global Grid Forum 5*, Edinburgh, July 2002.

[76] Napster Homepage. http://www.napster.com.

[77] Gnutella Homepage. http://www.gnutella.com.

[78] I. Stoica, R. Morris, D. Karger, M. F. Kaashoek, and H. Balakrishnan. Chord: A scalable peer-to-peer lookup service for internet applications. In *Proceedings of the 2001 conference on applications, technologies, architectures and protocols for computer communications*, San Diego, CA, August 2001. ACM.

[79] A. Rowstron and P. Druschel. *Pastry: Scalable Decentralized Object Location and Routing for Large-Scale Peer-to-Peer Systems*, volume 2218 of *Lecture Notes in Computer Science*, pages 329–350. 2001.

[80] S. Ratnasamy, P. Francis, M. Handley, R. Karp, and S. Schenker. A scalable content-addressable network. In *Proceedings of the 2001 conference on applications, technologies, architectures and protocols for computer communications*, San Diego, CA, August 2001. ACM.

[81] M. Harren, J. Hellerstein, R. Huebsch, B. T. Loo, Shenker S., and I. Stoica. Complex Queries in DHT-based Peer-to-Peer Networks. In *Proceedings of the 1st Internationsl Workshop on Peer-to-Peer Networks*, Cambridge, MA, March 2002.

[82] M. Noar and U. Wieder. Novel architectures for P2P applications: the continuous-discrete approach. In *Proceedings of the fifteenth annual ACM symposium on Parallel algorithms and architectures*, San Diego, CA, June 2003.

[83] Globus Toolkit. http://www.globus.org/toolkit/.

[84] Globus Toolkit 3.2. http://www.globus.org/toolkit/docs/3.2/.

Index

People

Dr. Franz-Josef Pfreundt

Fraunhofer Institut für Techno- und Wirtschaftsmathematik (ITWM), Germany

pfreundt@itwm.fhg.de

Franz-Josef Pfreundt studied Mathematics, Physics and Computer Science resulting in a Diploma in Mathematics and a Ph.D degree in Mathematical Physics (1986). From 1986-1995 he had a permanent position at the University of Kaiserslautern as Head of the Research Group for Industrial Mathematics. In 1995 he became Department Head of the Fraunhofer Institute for Industrial Mathematics - ITWM. His research topics are: Fluid dynamics, porous media, image analysis and parallel computing. At the ITWM he founded the departments: "Flow in complex structures" and "Models and algorithms in image analysis". Since 1999 he is Divison Director at Fraunhofer ITWM and Head of the "Competence Center for HPC and Visualization". In 2001 the prestigious Fraunhofer Research Prize was awarded to Franz-Josef Pfreundt, Konrad Steiner and their research group for their work on microstructure simulation.

Prof. Dr. Hans-Werner Meuer

IT Center, University of Mannheim

hans-werner.meuer@rz.uni-mannheim.de

Hans Meuer has studied mathematics, physics and politics at the universities of Marburg, Giessen and Vienna. In 1972, he received his doctorate in mathematics from the Rheinisch Westfälische Technical University (RWTH) of Aachen. Since 1974, he has been professor of mathematics and computer science at the University of Mannheim with specialization in software engineering. In 1986, he became co-founder and organizer of the first Mannheim Super Computer Seminar, which has been held annually ever since. In 1993, Hans Meuer started the TOP500 initiative together with Erich Strohmaier (previously at the University of Mannheim, currently at the NERSC) and Jack Dongarra (University of Tennessee and ORNL). In the TOP500 the most powerful computers in the world are listed ranked by their performance on the Linpack Benchmark. The list is updated twice a year. The first of these updates always coincides with the Mannheim/Heidelberg Supercomputer Conference in June, the second one is presented in November at the IEEE Super Computer Conference in the USA.

Dr.-Ing. habil. Alfred Geiger
T-Systems Solutions for Research GmbH
alfred.geiger@t-systems.com

Alfred Geiger is responsible for solution-management in simulation-technology and for service-management for customers from the aerospace segment at T-Systems - Solutions for Research. After studying aeronautical engineering he worked as a Ph.D.-student at the Institute for Aerodynamics and Gasdynamics of Stuttgart University. He joined the computing-center of Stuttgart University (RUS) in 1989 and established services and competence in parallel computing. From 1995 until 1999 he was head of the HPC-Center Stuttgart (HLRS), one of the few HPC-centers in Germany serving universities nationwide. In 2000 he joined debis Systemhaus, the service-organization of DaimlerChrysler (which was later acquired by T-Systems) as a service manager in Research and Education.

Prof. Dr.-Ing. habil. Djamshid Tavangarian
Chair of Computer Architecture, University of Rostock
djamshid.tavangarian@uni-rostock.de

Dr. Tavangarian is currently at the Department of CS & EE at the University of Rostock/Germany, where he represents the teaching and research area of Computer Architecture. He studied EE & IT at the Technical University of Berlin, finished his Ph.D. at the University of Dortmund and his professorship work at the University of Frankfurt/Germany in CS. After an industrial work at the Hewlett-Packard Company he worked at the University of Hagen/Germany and was responsible for the field of computer architecture and design of integrated circuits. Connected with research contracts he worked at the Universities of Berkeley (UCB) and Santa Barbara (UCSB) in the USA, too. The current main topics of his research activities concentrate on computer architectures for local area and wide area computing systems, embedded systems, wireless communication systems as well as Multimedia architectures for mobile learning. He consulted the Ministries and governmental institutions in Germany in the field of mobile learning and is author and co-author of more than 200 scientific publications (books, book chapters, journals and conference articles). He is member of several scientific organizations.

Giovanni Falcone
IT Center, University of Mannheim
falcone@rz.uni-mannheim.de

Giovanni Falcone obtained his "Diplom" (equivalent to MSc degree) in computer science form the University of Mannheim, Germany in 2004. Presently, he is a doctoral candidate in the Department of Maths and Computer Science at the University of Mannheim. His current research interests are in the area of software engineering and software reuse.

Dr. Heinz Kredel
IT Center, University of Mannheim
kredel@rz.uni-mannheim.de

Heinz Kredel got his "Diplom" (equivalent to MSc degree) in Mathematics from the University of Heidelberg and received his doctorate in Mathematics and Computer Science from the University of Passau. At present, he is leading the working group 'Zentrale Systeme' together with W. Aufsattler at the IT Center of the University of Mannheim. He has been working in the areas of computer system administration and computer algebra with special focus on parallel computation and software development for more than twenty years.

Sebastien Kreuter
IT Center, University of Mannheim
skreuter@rumms.uni-rostock.de

Sebastien Kreuter, student of computer science at the University of Mannheim, works sience 2004 as student assistant for the IPACS project at the IT-Center.

Michael Krietemeyer
Chair of Computer Architecture, University of Rostock
michael.krietemeyer@uni-rostock.de

Michael Krietemeyer got his graduate degree in Technical Computer Science from the University of Rostock in 2004. Thenceforward he works at the Chair of Computer Architecture on the IPACS project.

Dr. Dirk Merten
Fraunhofer Institut für Techno- und Wirtschaftsmathematik
(ITWM), Germany
merten@itwm.fhg.de

Dirk Merten has studied physics and mathematics at the University of Bonn and received his doctorate in physics in 2002 from the Helmholtz-Institut für Strahlen- und Kernphysik of the University of Bonn, Germany. Since 2003 he is Scientist at the Competence Center for High Performance Computing and Visualization at the Fraunhofer-Institut für Techno- und Wirtschaftsmathematik, Kaiserslautern, Germany 1998-2002 Doctoral student at the University of Bonn, Germany. His main interests are parallel computing, performance characterization and Benchmarking.

Martin Meuer
IT Center, University of Mannheim
martin.meuer@rz.uni-mannheim.de

Martin Meuer holds a graduate degree in Computer Science from the University of Karlsruhe, Germany. Martin has worked for FRZ and Controlware as IT security consultant before he joined the IPACS project. He is now the Asscociate Director of Prometeus, organizer of the International Supercomputer Conference and promoter of the TOP500 supercomputer lists.

Matthias Merz
IT Center, University of Mannheim
merz@rz.uni-mannheim.de

Matthias Merz received his "Diplom" (equivalent to MSc degree) in computer science and business administration from the University of Mannheim (Germany) in 2002. Since then, he has been working as a research assistant at the University of Mannheim on the IPACS project. At the IT-Center, he has been responsible for the campus-wide SAP-R/3 administration for more than three years. He is currently completing his PhD studies in computer science at the University of Mannheim, department of Information Systems III. His main research interests focus on persistence frameworks, especially on the Java Data Objects specification (JDO).

David Reinig

IT Center, University of Mannheim

dreinig@rz.uni-mannheim.de

David Reinig is an apprentice at the University of Mannheim IT-Center. His task in the IPACS project was the graphical visualization of the benchmark results on the Web Page. In addition he wrote tools for managing the database.

Henry Ristau

Chair of Computer Architecture, University of Rostock

henry.ristau@uni-rostock.de

Henry Ristau studied computer engineering and medical informatics at the Fachhochschule Stralsund - University of Applied Sciences and received his graduate degree in computer engineering in 2002. From 2002 to 2003 he worked for Quasa gGmbH at the development of an internet-based quality assurance registry. Afterwards he studied technical computer science at the University of Rostock where he received his graduate degree in computer science in 2004. Since 2005 he works at the Chair of Computer Architecture at the University of Rostock. In addition to the IPACS project, where his research topics were distributed systems and distributed storage technologies, his interests include networking, protocols and load-balancing as much as the development of hard- and software for embedded systems.

Dr. Christian Simmendinger

T-Systems Solutions for Research GmbH

christian.simmendinger@t-systems-sfr.com

Christian Simmendinger is working as a HPC consultant for T-Systems - Solutions for Research. After studying physics he worked as a Ph.D.-student at the Institute for Theoretical Physics at the University of Stuttgart. As a research fellow in the area of numerical simulation he worked for the Institute of Physics at the VU Amsterdam and the University of Carlos III in Madrid. In 2000 he joined debis Systemhaus, the service-organization of DaimlerChrysler, which was later acquired by T-Systems.

 **Daniel Versick**

Chair of Computer Architecture, University of Rostock

daniel.versick@uni-rostock.de
Daniel Versick studied technical computer science at the University of Rostock and received his graduate degree in computer science in 2004. Since then, he is working as a research assistant at the Chair of Computer Architecture at the University of Rostock. Besides the IPACS project his research interests include the development of hard- and software for embedded systems and realtime systems.